vine to bottle

vine to bottle

how wine is made

simon woods

photography by jason lowe

mitchell beazley

Vine to Bottle
by Simon Woods
with photography by Jason Lowe

First published in Great Britain in 2001 by
Mitchell Beazley, an imprint of Octopus Publishing
Group Limited, 2–4 Heron Quays, London E14 4JP.

A CIP catalogue record for this book is available
from the British Library.

ISBN: 1 84000 339 1

Commissioning Editor: Rebecca Spry
Executive Art Editor: Philip Ormerod, Tracy Killick
Managing Editors: Hilary Lumsden, Jamie Grafton
Design: Paul Reid and Lloyd Tilbury at Cobalt ID
Editors: Adrian Tempany, Julia Harding
Proofreader: Susan Keevil
Production: Jessame Emms
Index: John Noble
Typeset in Rotis Sans Serif
Printed and bound by Toppan Printing Company
in China

contents

Acknowledgements

This book would never have been written without the help
of several people.

To all at Maison Louis Jadot (the names of some of whom
have been changed for this book), but especially Paquito Barbier,
Christine Botton, Pierre-Henry Gagey, Claude Hilt, Jacques
Lardière and Hubert Naus – thank you for your patience,
generosity and of course your delicious wines.

To Ashley Huntington of Domaine de la Baume – thank you
for the benefit of your knowledge and opinions, especially
those concerning wild yeasts.

To Rosamund Hitchcock of R & R Teamwork; Brett Fleming of
BRL Hardy Europe; and Patrick McGrath, Lyn Murray, Philip Tuck
of Hatch Mansfield – thank you for lightening my burdens just
when I needed it.

To Jason Lowe – thank you for introducing me to the Citroën Maserati
and the Tequila Stuntman. Oh, and the pics were quite good too.

To Rebecca Spry, Hilary Lumsden and Jamie Grafton of Mitchell
Beazley – thank you for your constant encouragement and the
flexibility of your deadlines.

Finally to my two ladies, Jill and Isabella, with love and apologies.
I'm back now.

Introduction

Why? It's a question I've been asking ever since I found myself buying wine for its flavour rather than its effect. Why does one patch of land produce a wine which is so majestic, when a seemingly identical plot can only manage something a tenth as compelling? Why can one winemaker regularly turn out bottles which thrill, when his neighbour struggles to make something drinkable, even in the best of vintages? Why do two different barrels of what should in theory be the same wine taste different? Why does wine A sell for £3 while wine B can command £300?

I'd like to say that this book answers all these questions and more. It doesn't. There's no one formula for making either good wine or bad wine. Scientific research can help us understand more about the processes of grape growing and wine making, but it can never explain the difference between something that is great, and something that is merely very good. I find it immensely comforting that several of the world's finest winemakers admit to following particular practices '... because that's what works best'.

What the book does do is look at the decisions which those involved in turning a bunch of grapes into a bottle of wine have to make in the course of a typical year. The view is through the eyes of one particular producer, Maison Louis Jadot of Burgundy. Photographer Jason Lowe and I visited Jadot several times in the run up to the 2000 harvest, and we've tried to capture in words and pictures the processes and personalities involved.

You'll be introduced to Jacques Lardière, Jadot's twinkling cellar master - the French have no word for 'winemaker' - and his bustling second-in-command, Christine. You'll meet the immaculately groomed Pierre-Henry Gagey who runs the company for its owners, a trio of American sisters, and is also in charge of work in the vineyards, the day-to-day execution of which falls to a team headed by Claude Hilt. And you'll also make the acquaintance of several members of the boisterous picking crew.

This book also shows how Ashley Huntingdon of Domaine de la Baume, the high-tech Languedoc winery owned by Australian giant BRL Hardy, tackles a year in the vineyard and the winery. The approaches of Jadot and La Baume are often quite different, and their styles of wines are certainly very different. Why? Read on...

raw materials

'I believe that the potential of "terroir" and microclimate can be realised in vineyards the world over, as long as you grow the grape variety that best suits the soil. But it is the winemaker's skill that turns excellent fruit into fine wine.'

ERNIE LOOSEN, GERMAN WINEMAKER

Suppose you have two bottles of Pinot Noir. Both have come from the same region and have been produced using the same techniques. But the wines taste completely different. Why? Because they are made from grapes grown in different vineyards, which have different *terroir*. Pronounced 'terr-wahhh', so the second syllable oozes from your lips, *terroir* roughly translates as 'soil–aspect–gradient–altitude–climate–geography'. It is most easily defined as all the things over which the winemaker has no control. But it can make a wine divine – or a disaster.

Burgundy is an excellent place to study terroir. The locals have spent centuries mapping out the best bits and in the Côte d'Or, the heart of the region, there are literally hundreds of delineated vineyards, each of which is supposed to produce a wine different in some significant way from its neighbour. Top sites can sometimes command prices ten, even a hundred times higher than less favoured ones. Cynics – of which there are plenty where terroir is concerned – say that this is just pulling the wool over the eyes of gullible wine drinkers, and that it is the winemaker who exerts the biggest influence on a wine. If that's true, why then is Jacques Lardière's Beaune Grèves noticeably different from his Beaune Teurons, which comes from the vineyard next door? And why does his Auxey-Duresses taste of roof tiles?

The lie of the land
Of the many factors in terroir, landscape is the most visible. It's not hard to see a world of difference between the vast, flat prairies of vineyards in Australia's Riverland and the sharp slopes overlooking

the Mosel in Germany, although Riesling grapes flourish on both. Four factors come into play in the vineyard landscape: aspect, gradient, altitude and local geography. First, aspect.

Professional sunbathers know that they'll tan fastest by facing into the sun as directly as possible. Vines are fixed to the spot, so they can't ape such mobile measures, but in cool regions where there is a need to maximise sun exposure they can be planted to ensure that they receive sunlight for as much of the day as possible. In the northern hemisphere this means siting them on slopes which face south-to-southeast (as in Burgundy's Côte d'Or), or north-to-northeast in the southern hemisphere. They receive the first rays of sun in the morning and are still casting shadows late into the evening, when neighbouring sites have bitten the dusk. Growers in much warmer areas where the sunlight is more intense often prefer to site their vines so they face away from the midday sun.

The gradient of vineyards varies from flat to almost suicidal. Again, think of our sunbather, who inclines her lounger to receive more of the sun's rays when the orange orb isn't especially high in

'In Burgundy, the locals have spent centuries mapping out the best bits of land. There are hundreds of delineated vineyards, each of which is supposed to make a wine that's significantly different from its neighbour'.

the sky. A reasonably accurate rule of thumb is that the cooler the spot, the steeper the slope – hence the vertiginous vineyards ranged along the northern banks of the Mosel river, which would make a trailblazing goat tread with caution.

Slopes also mean that excess rainwater drains off more quickly after a downpour. Water isn't the only thing which drains off. Freezing air in spring can wreak havoc when the vines are flowering (see Chapter Two), but on sites with an incline it can flow away down the slope, reducing the incidence of frost damage. The effects of altitude are simple: higher equals cooler, lower equals warmer.

There are several ways in which local geography can influence the terroir. Rocks can store up heat during the day and radiate it at night. Bodies of water tone down the extremes of temperature and can also reflect the sun onto the vines. And trees close to vineyards can provide shelter from wind, rain and hail. The only portion of the Jadot vineyards to be affected by a hailstorm in August 2000 was in Marsannay, where the storm found its way through a gap in the forest which runs along the western edge of the Côte d'Or.

Weather or not?

Climate is as complex a topic as landscape, so let's first establish what climate is not: climate is not weather. Each evening, millions of Britons watch the forecast at the end of the news in the hope that tomorrow will be sunny. That is weather. Each year, millions of

Britons go on holiday to the Costa del Sol, because they know that the chances of the sun shining continuously for a fortnight in Clacton in July are pretty slim. That is climate. Climate is the norm, and weather is the variation from that norm.

Grapes can grow in a wide variety of climates, with different varieties requiring different conditions. In Burgundy, the range of varieties is limited by the appellation authorities, and with a few exceptions boils down to Pinot Noir for reds and Chardonnay for whites. In most vineyards, the planting decision is easy. No-one would think of planting Chardonnay in the great red vineyard of Le Chambertin, just as it would be foolish to grow Pinot in Le Montrachet, source of arguably the finest white wine in the world.

However, a few villages, especially in the north of the Côte de Beaune, can turn out reds and whites with equal success. Pierre-Henry Gagey points out the Jadot holdings on the hill of Corton, the only grand cru site for both red and white burgundy. Jadot grows Pinot on the upper slopes and Chardonnay lower down. 'Lots of places can make great red wine, but few can make whites to match Burgundy. If we were driven by economics, this would be all white wine, since [white] Corton-Charlemagne commands twice the price of [red] Corton-Pougets. But we like the red.

But whether it's Pinot Noir or Chardonnay, there are three things which no vine can survive without: heat, sunlight and water. Heat in spring is required to stir the vines from their winter slumbers, ideally

LA BAUME

TERROIR'S TURN
'Soil is dirt', was the famous cry from an Australian commentator not so very long ago. Indeed throughout the 1970s and 1980s, the word 'terroir' was considered a swear word in many New World wineries, with the winemaker receiving all the adulation. Many are now changing their mind, and La Baume winemaker Ashley certainly doesn't underestimate the vineyard's influence in the quality of a wine. 'I don't use the term "terroir", as it seems to imply everything is at the whim of the gods. Wherever you are, you can't make good wine unless you have fundamentally good vineyards, governed by good management practices. The days of rock-star winemakers are thankfully disappearing, and many producers are now realising that the guy in the vineyard is just as important.'

LA BAUME

MARRIED OR SINGLE

'We've done 11 vintages now at Domaine de la Baume, and I'm still coming to terms with the huge range of soils,' says Ashley. 'It's difficult to look at something and say "That's a good soil" or "That's a bad soil", since what works with one variety may be unsuitable for another. We're finding that some grapes such as Syrah are incredibly sensitive as to where they grow but others, Merlot and Chardonnay for instance, are much more flexible. With Chardonnay there's a big difference in the wines you get from the various sites. Normally we've blended these together, but we're now moving towards using selected vineyards for some of the better wines. Our Chardonnay Sélection is a blend from just two sites, one of which gives a forward, fruity style, while the other is finer and leaner, and provides structure.'

in unison (so they all ripen at the same time) and not so early that they become prone to late frosts. However, the critical time for a successful vine is during the ripening period from veraison (see page 35) to harvest, when the mean temperature should be between 15 and 21°C, depending on the grape variety. Below this level the grapes' acidity will be high and they may not even ripen. Above this level the acidity will be too low, resulting in flabby wines.

Cool your roots, man

Many parts of the world seem on first inspection to be too hot to grow vines. However, there will often be something which serves to temper the torrid heat, perhaps chilly nights – during which ripening ceases – or the occasional daytime sea breeze, mist or fog which cools the vines. Heat and sunlight are related, but they weave different patterns. Sunlight is essential for photosynthesis, the process by which a grape accumulates the sugar that will eventually convert to alcohol. While this makes it a restrictive factor on vine growth, most regions which are warm enough to ripen grapes have more than adequate sunlight. An adverse effect of too much sun is that, just like humans, grapes can suffer from sunburn. There's no bottles of factor 25 to be slapped on these little fellas, but decent canopy management (see Chapter 2) can help shade these grapes from the worst excesses of the sun.

Water is the third essential ingredient of climate; no surprise there, as it makes up more than 80 per cent of virtually every wine. Traditional regions receive their water in the form of rainfall, which can be a blessing or a curse depending on when it falls. Winter rain

replenishes underground water supplies, while gentle showers through spring and summer give succour to thirsty vines and ensure they don't suffer from water stress when photosynthesis ceases to occur. However, heavy rain and hail are unwelcome at any point in the growing season and especially in the ripening period, when they shred leaves and split grape skins, leaving them prone to rot. Rain prior to harvest is not as catastrophic, but it does mean that the wines will be more dilute.

Wet and windy

With irrigation at the grower's disposal the picture changes somewhat. First, it means that regions which were considered too dry for viticulture can now be developed. But irrigation can also benefit established vineyards, providing much-needed moisture at a time when the vineyards are vulnerable to water stress.

Another important aspect of climate is wind, which like rainfall can be both a good thing and a bad thing. Breezes blowing through the vineyards help dry the leaves after rain, reducing the incidence of fungal diseases and having a cooling effect. They are a good thing. Heavy gusts, on the other hand, can rip leaves and shoots off vines, especially young ones. They are a bad thing, and trees are often planted nearby to act as windbreaks.

'There is little scientific evidence that soil minerals can be transmitted to a wine. But why does Mosel Riesling often taste of slate, and Santorini's Assyrtiko wines of the local volcanic rock?'

Back in Beaune, Jacques Lardière is convinced that the 'macro-molecular activity' in the soils of Burgundy is speaking out in his wines. 'Wine is about fermentation *and* mutation', he says. 'You need to transmit what was in the soil – the silica, the quartz and everything else – into the bottle.'

Soil is just one part of the terroir equation, but its importance varies depending on where you come from. Europeans often think like Jacques, that soils give particular characters to each wine. To many producers in other parts of the world, soil is only there to stand the vines in, while admittedly providing them with something to drink and a few nutrients at a satisfactory pace. There's little scientific evidence that any of the minerals present in soils can be transmitted to the wine. But why does Mosel Riesling often taste of slate, and why do wines made from the Assyrtiko grape on the island of Santorini have the sulphury tang of the local volcanic rock?

While the debate over precisely what flavours the soil brings to a wine will rumble on for many years, what isn't in doubt is the importance of soil structure. The best soils are those which are fairly deep, well-drained, not too heavy and not especially fertile, but with enough organic matter to provide some food for both vines and worms. Soil colour also has an effect. Darker soils absorb heat during the day and then radiate it at night, while light soils reflect the sun's rays onto the vines.

Landscape, climate, soil... The many variations in each mean that there's no such thing as typical terroir. And considering there's no such thing as a typical wine, that's just as it should be.

LA BAUME

LEGACY OF THE LANGUEDOC
Will the Languedoc ever be mapped out as precisely as Burgundy? Probably not. The vineyards of southern France are amazingly diverse, which is what makes them such an exciting prospect for the future. Chardonnay isn't the only Burgundian variety to thrive. A testimony to the potential of Pinot Noir is that the firm of Antonin Rodet in Burgundy has recently (August 2000) acquired an estate near Limoux, where it plans to produce upmarket Pinot. With land costing 10% of a mediocre Côte d'Or site, who can blame them?

Opposite. Not the world's largest corkscrew. *The large drill is for breaking up the soil and root systems when vines are replanted*

Below left. Out with the old... *As a result of diseases and old age, it's a rare vineyard which boasts vines older then 50 years*

Below right. ...And in with the new

the vine

'To understand the vine, look at its origins as a forest dweller. Sunlight triggers a 15-month reproductive cycle, and it is sunlight penetration of the summer canopy that fuels photosynthesis, resulting in the final ripe grapes and ripe seed tannins.'

JAMES HALLIDAY, AUSTRALIAN WINEMAKER

Few crops cover as much of the planet as grape vines. Yet even in the best terroir, getting a grape to turn out good wine calls for skill, patience and strategy. No wonder opinions on viticulture differ so starkly around the world, and even within regions. The vine has a near-monopoly on parts of Burgundy's landscape, but each vineyard is unique to the trained eye. Spot a sprawling mass of leaves and shoots and you've found a vine grower more interested in hunting than in viticulture, while next door the super-manicured vines suggest the anally-retentive are at work.

Above and right. Smokin'. *The burning of winter prunings provides fertiliser for the vineyards and much needed warmth for the pruners*

Pierre-Henry Gagey is one of those stylish continental types who probably look suave in their pyjamas. Maison Jadot is owned by a trio of American sisters, but the task of managing it is left to Pierre-Henry, who took over that role from his late father André in 1992. He travels extensively to promote his wines but is happiest when in Beaune. 'My love is the production of wine. Jacques Lardière makes it happen in the winery, but we need to do a good job in the vineyards, and that is my responsibility.'

It's a responsibility he takes very seriously. However, his other roles mean that he can't spend his time pruning and ploughing, so he leaves much of the day-to-day running of the vineyards to Claude Hilt. Jason (the intrepid photographer) and I always seem to meet Claude before 8am, when his aftershave (like a Conran restaurant toilet, according to Jason) is at its most pungent. On this particular morning, he and his team will be replanting some dead or dying vines in Clos Vougeot with new ones.

But while it is certainly Pinot Noir that will be going into the ground, Claude can't just go to the vine shop and say: 'Two dozen Pinot Noir vines, *s'il vous plaît*.' First of all, there's the question of which clone of Pinot Noir to plant. Clonal selection has been practised in Burgundy for donkeys' years, albeit on an unscientific

basis. Growers would notice which of their vines performed best, and when it was time to replant they would use cuttings from these plants. The scientists got involved from 1960 onwards, at a time when the fan-leaf virus was having a debilitating effect on Chardonnay in particular. They were able to isolate virus-free clones, which were then approved by the local authorities, propagated and made available to growers. The problem, only discovered after many growers had replanted their vineyards, was that these new clones, though healthy, produced rather ordinary wines. It wasn't until the 1990s that there was a selection of clones available which had been chosen for their quality and their disease-resistance.

Beating the bug

Claude now buys all his plants, and each year he's been sending a selection to a nursery near Dijon in order to build up a library of special Jadot plant matter. But there is not one single Jadot Pinot clone. Diversity is crucial in producing complex wines, and the plan is to have a wide range of different clones to choose from.

The next stage is planting the selected clone, right? Wrong. You could do that, but it would fall prey to phylloxera in next to no time. In the last half of the 19th century the phylloxera beetle arrived

LA BAUME

GOOD WINE NEEDS NO BUSH
Many of the vines from which
Ashley sources fruit are what are
known as bush vines, in other
words free-standing vines with
short trunks and no trellising
system. It's the traditional way of
growing them, and for some
varieties in certain vineyards, it's
still the best system. 'Trying to
update some of them would be
superfluous and a complete waste
of money,' says Ashley, 'so I won't.'

from its native America and began munching its way through the
vineyards of Europe, destroying virtually everything in its path. The
eventual solution was to graft the European vines (*Vitis vinifera*)
onto rootstocks of American vines, which had evolved alongside
phylloxera and thus were resistant to it.

A grafted vine costs substantially more than a simple cutting
straight from the vineyard, not least because there's a wait of a year
from the time of grafting until it is ready to plant out. But since the
alternative is no wine at all, the producers have no option but to pay
up. As with clones, there's now a wide variety of rootstocks; some of
which affect the vigour of a vine, while others improve its tolerance
to high lime or salt levels in the soil. And there are others resistant
to prolonged periods of drought.

Trials are also underway into genetically modified rootstocks that
are resistant to various diseases, although this news has received
a mixed reception in Burgundy. Indeed in July 2000, Pierre-Henry
and Jacques were co-signatories along with several other eminent

Burgundians to a document requesting a minimum ten-year moratorium on any GMO vine and wine marketing, as well as a re-orientation and total transparency in research and approval procedures. 'We've noted that many questions remain unanswered: a decrease in the genetic diversity of our grape varieties, the risk of loss of typicity in our wines, of environmental dissemination and other unforeseeable and irreversible consequences.'

Fanatical botanical

Having selected which rootstock and which Pinot clone are appropriate for the relevant vineyard, Claude is now ready to begin planting. After the old stump has been turfed out, a half-man sized corkscrew-like implement is brought out of the shed and set to work, digging a new hole and breaking up the surrounding earth. With the new ground cleared, the vine is inserted and fitted with a plastic collar to protect it from the worst of the weather.

Replanting one or two vines in a vineyard is fairly routine stuff, but replanting the entire plot involves a little more thought. Over many years the Burgundians have toyed with many different ways of organising their vineyards, and even now there's no consensus as to the best method. There are a number of issues to consider. The soil here tends to be relatively infertile, so few vines will produce

Right. Hard graft. *A grafted vine is given a final trim before planting*

Far right. Practice safe viticulture. *A fledgling vine puts forth its first shoots within its protective plastic jacket*

LA BAUME

POPULAR MECHANICALS

Ashley's Australian background cannot be transported direct to the Languedoc. 'Back home, we plant Shiraz [known in France as Syrah] with about 2,000 plants per hectare, but here with the less vigorous soils, the norm is much higher than that. We've just planted a Syrah vineyard with 4,000 vines per hectare which is standard round here, but the main difference between our vineyard and others in the region is that ours has been established with mechanisation in mind. We still do the pruning by hand, but pruning is only one stage in a year-long procedure. Thanks to the trellising system, we can do jobs such as pre-pruning [trimming the vines prior to a full pruning], foliage management and wire-lifting by machine, which saves us lots of time and effort.'

a huge amount of foliage, which could shade its neighbour. But while this means that the vines can be quite close together, they still need to be far enough apart to let the early morning and late afternoon sun shine over the adjacent row onto the grapes – and to let a tractor through. The typical Burgundian spacing is for both the rows and the vines along those rows to be one metre apart.

The vines need to get as much sunlight as possible, which also sets an upper limit on the height to which they will be trained, while the weather sets the lower limit – the vines need to be high enough to avoid being nipped by ground frosts. This means that the grapes hang down around knee level, which doesn't do much for the backs of the pruners and pickers.

Vines aren't the only thing grown here: grass is often evident between every other row, in part to limit the vine's vigour as it competes for root space, but also, on sloping sites, to minimise soil

Right. Tie and dry - *Last year's canes have been tied together for neatness and ease of pruning using the highest of hi-tech material...*

erosion. Sometimes you'll also find roses at the end of the rows, which isn't just for aesthetic reasons: if they start looking unhealthy, it's an early-warning sign that powdery mildew could be set to strike.

Prozac, anyone?

It's October, and the harvest has finished. The leaves still cling to the vines, but their plump, green summer vigour has been replaced by the rustling yellow, gold and brown of autumn. With each gust of wind a few more tumble to the floor, although it takes the first sharp frost to really strip the foliage. After the mayhem of vintage the vineyards are calm once more, but for the next few weeks there's still work to be done tidying the vineyards, ploughing between the rows and spreading fertiliser. In all vineyards – in one of those processes only the French could name, *buttage* – the soil is banked up at the base of the vines to protect them from frost.

Below. The world's narrowest lawn?
Grass is often grown between the vines in order to reduce vigour. Here, it is between every other row

Come December, the last leaves have fallen and the vines have entered their dormant stage, which will last through until budbreak in spring. With the vineyard looking as bare as at any time of the year, this is the best time to check the trellising system and replace any wires or posts that have been damaged.

The most important task in winter, however, is pruning. This needs to be done before budbreak, otherwise the new buds could suffer at the hands of clumsy pruners. Why prune? It's not just to keep the vineyard tidy, although in the tightly spaced rows of the Côte d'Or this is important. The point behind pruning is to limit the yield for the following vintage, by reducing the number of buds that will subsequently become bunches of grapes.

Meet the patron saint of pruning

The traditional day for Burgundians to start pruning is St Vincent's Day, 22 January, but with such an extensive domaine to oversee the task occupies most of the winter months for Claude and his team. In the cold air, mist and smoke mingle. Some of the latter spirals from the cigarettes wedged into the pruners' mouths, but most comes from the rickety old wheelbarrows-cum-braziers that are pushed up the row in the pruners' wake to burn the cuttings. The bottom of the barrow has a grate through which the ash falls, scattering organic matter across the vineyards. Not all the prunings are burnt, as it's now time to take cuttings for propagation.

LA BAUME

WATER, WATER EVERYWHERE
'We just want to produce healthy vines.' Irrigation isn't permitted in any of France's appellation contrôlée vineyards, but since La Baume's wines fall into the vin de pays category, Ashley is able to water as and when he wants (water supplies permitting). To do this, each row of vines has a black tube with holes at strategic intervals through which water can be pumped whenever it is required. 'It's not a case of turning the system on at the same time every day or every week. We look at what the weather's been like and decide what the vines need. For example, 1998 was a drought year, and if we hadn't used the irrigation, the grapes wouldn't have ripened properly, and the yield would have been lousy. In 1999 however, we hardly turned it on at all.'

Left. Snipped in the bud. *For pruning, no machine can match a skilled pair of hands and a shiny new pair of secateurs*

As winter turns over to early spring the ground warms up and the sap begins to rise in the vines. Indeed, water can often be seen oozing out of the pruning scars. Soon, the buds left after the pruning begin to swell and eventually, out of each (hopefully) pops the tip of a tender green shoot. But this tenderness means that it is prey to frosts, and once these have struck it's bye-bye bud.

The Chardonnay and Pinot Noir that populate Burgundy are early ripeners in the grape world and, thus, especially sensitive to frost. The gentle slope of the Côte d'Or means that much of the cold air funnels off the well-sited vineyards, but with the threat of chilly spells lasting until May this is still a nerve-wracking time. In some vineyards there are large wind machines on hand to stir up the cold surface air and mix it with warmer, higher air.

Over here sun, on me head

With the vine kicking off its growing cycle, it's time for *debuttage* – yes, removing the banked-up soil – followed by a light ploughing in order to aerate the base of the vines. Spring is also the time to plant new vines, preferably when the ground has dried out slightly, otherwise the roots are at risk of rotting.

Above. Early days. *The first signs of a cluster of buds breaking through. Frost at this point makes normally reticent growers swear loudly*

The shoots grow slowly at first, relying on the carbohydrates stored in the vine for their food. Then, as their leaves develop, the process of photosynthesis gets underway, in which carbon dioxide and water are transformed into sugar and oxygen. This is powered by light energy from the sun and at this stage the shoot growth is rapid – as much as three centimetres a day – so it's important that the main canes have been attached to the trellis wires before this stage. The shoots themselves are positioned between two horizontal wires for neatness and because it will make subsequent operations that much easier.

Providing there's not too much rainfall, the shoot vigour begins to diminish as spring turns into summer. Over this period, a few small, button-like clusters will have been appearing on the shoots, and these eventually develop into individual flowers. Every stage in the year's harvest is critical, but few more immediately so than this, as it is now that flowering and fruit set will take place. The rather unsightly flowers open up to release their pollen and try to fertilise themselves as well as their neighbours (vines for most wines are hermaphroditic). Successful coupling will result in fruit set and then a baby grape is born. But the celebrations must wait.

'The gentle slope of the Côte d'Or allows cold air to funnel away from the well-sited vineyards. But this is still a nerve-wracking time, with the threat of chilly spells lasting until May.'

the grape

'The grape is the beautiful warehouse of all the elements the vine creates before harvest – sugar, acid, pectin, tannins and aromas – along with the water and minerals that the roots extract from the earth. This marvellous alchemy has allowed mankind to extract the best from the sky and the earth for thousands of years.'
MIGUEL TORRES, SPANISH WINEMAKER

It's May, and Claude is nervous. In fact, everyone in Burgundy is nervous. The weather so far this year has been favourable, so the vines have been roused from their winter slumbers a fortnight earlier than usual. For the last few weeks they've been stretching their new leaves and tendrils into the milder atmosphere and have reached that critical stage – flowering. A sharp frost now could wreck the vintage, and everywhere you look people are chewing their fingernails. There's nothing the growers can do now but wait, hope and pray.

'Claude has been almost too lucky this year, as the potential crop is huge. It's doubtful whether the vines will ripen into top-notch wine.'

Cold, damp weather at this time means that the fruit set will be erratic, and this can have a dramatic effect on the eventual yield, although not necessarily on quality. But Claude has been lucky. May was fine, and the vines flowered and set a large, healthy crop of fruit in fine, warm conditions. Baby grapes – tough, a shocking green and a fraction of their eventual size – jut forth from the stalks in angry clusters. Try tasting one. Yuk. This may be a grape from the famous Chevalier-Montrachet vineyard, but at this pre-pubescent stage it is ten times more tart than an unripe gooseberry.

If anything Claude has been too lucky this year, as the potential crop is huge. Even if the good weather continues until harvest, it's doubtful whether the vines will be able to ripen all their grapes to the level required for top-notch wine. This means carrying out a *vendange verte* (green harvest); in other words, going through each vineyard and snipping off some bunches from those vines that appear to be especially heavily laden.

The vine is at its most vigorous straight after fruit set and thinning out the crop at this stage would merely force the vine into putting extra effort into producing yet more foliage. Claude usually waits another couple of months until veraison (more later), in July, before sending his team out with the secateurs, by which time the growth has calmed down. (While *vendange verte* can be done after veraison, it shouldn't be delayed too long, otherwise the vine will expend a significant proportion of its energy on bunches of grapes which end up being lopped off.) Whether or not it is the size of the

Right. Hail but not hearty. *It looks like an insect's been chomping this leaf, but it's the effects of hail*

LA BAUME

ANYONE FOR CANOPIES?
'I get annoyed when people trot out the old "a vine has to struggle" maxim. It's complete... is this going into print?... OK then, it's complete twaddle.'
So what's Ashley's goal in the vineyards? 'The important thing is to create a balanced vine, and you do this through canopy management, changing the exposure of the fruit to the sun, altering the ratio of fruit to leaves. Quite what you do varies from site to site, depending on the fertility of the soil, the microclimate and the variety. And after a while, you can just look at a vine and know whether or not it's in balance. If it's stressed, it's not good, and if it's too vigorous, it's not good.'

2000 vintage that has caught people on the hop, a few growers can still be seen wandering around their vineyards snipping off excess bunches just three weeks before harvest begins. Their efforts will reduce the quantity, but have only a minimal effect on quality.

Veraison marks the time when the grape, which has now grown to roughly half its ultimate size, begins to ripen. The most visible sign of new arrival is the transformation of its skin colour from chlorophyll-stuffed green to reddish-purple or golden-yellow. There's change taking place inside the skin, too, as the sugar starts to accumulate and the acidity drops steadily.

Even within the same vineyard, veraison will start at different times for different vines. In fact, you'll find bunches in which some grapes have changed colour while others remain green for a few more days. Those which face the sun tend to develop earlier than

Above. Leaf it out. *Machines strip away foliage leaving grapes open to sunlight and the flow of air. Improvements in canopy management have also led to a reduction in the use of insecticides*

those on the opposite side of the bunch, and there's not much a vineyard manager like Claude can do about this. However, there are measures he can take to ensure that the grapes receive the optimum exposure to sunlight, and these – along with a number of other vineyard practices – fall under a blanket heading...

Canopy management

It's a phrase to drop into wine-y conversations to make others think you know what you're talking about. Its aims are to influence the quantity and quality of grapes produced and minimise the risk of disease. Volumes have been written on the subject and apparently make fascinating reading, at least to those who enjoy such things.

For each bunch of grapes, a vine needs a certain amount of leaves, to get the desired level of sugar-boosting photosynthesis. Pinot Noir in particular likes a high leaf-to-fruit ratio, as the pros would say. It's important that these leaves don't provide too much shade for the fruit; partly because a sprawling vine with large amounts of foliage acts as a mini-greenhouse, creating humid conditions in which fungal diseases can thrive. But it's also because insufficient sunlight inhibits phenolic ripeness. *Que?*

Phenolic ripeness relates to (among other things) colour, tannin and flavour compounds, and it's just as important – maybe even more important – to have phenolic ripeness as sugar ripeness. Good exposure to sunlight of the grapes and the canes (the wine word for branches) on which they grow is essential for phenolic ripeness.

In the low fertility soils of Burgundy, huge amounts of foliage are rare, so canopy management is reasonably straightforward. Even so, a look around the vineyards quickly reveals those growers who deem it unimportant: unfortunately, their wines often provide evidence of how wrong they are. Claude's vines are, like the man himself, neatly trimmed (but minus the aftershave). The branches with leaves are trained upwards between two foliage wires, while the fruit hangs down, allowing air to circulate around it.

There may be no Paco Rabanne among the Jadot vines, but they do receive a selection of feeds and sprays throughout the year in order to maintain their overall well-being. Throughout Burgundy there is now a realisation that many of the chemical treatments used from the 1950s onwards had a negative influence on the vines' health. The growers turned to artificial fertilisers in the first place because with the gradual decline in cattle farming on the Côte d'Or after the war, manure became harder to obtain. The new treatments may have stimulated vine growth, but they also had their side-effects. Fortunately, a pure coincidence obviously, the fertiliser salesmen also had products which would cure these unwanted side-effects, along with others which would deal with encroaching weeds and marauding insects. Which, of course, also had some side-effects.

Desert wines

It wasn't long before the vines became trapped in a vicious circle of what was, in effect, drug addiction. Rather than stretching their roots down to search for nutrients in the soil, they would develop

GERM-FREE ADOLESCENT
'When I hear my friends in Australia complain about diseases, I tell them they don't know what they're talking about,' sighs Ashley. The Languedoc enjoys one of the warmest, driest climates in France but problems still abound. 'It's all the usual suspects – botrytis, mildew of various sorts, the lot. People seem to think we're immune because we're in the south, but it doesn't work like that. It's the variability in the climate which causes the diseases. It can be hot for a week, after which it cools down and there's some rain. But the next day, the sun's out again, and the humidity soars. So too does the rot.'

'One of France's top soil scientists claims that at the start of the 1990s, many Côte d'Or vineyards showed less microbial activity than the Sahara.'

shallow root structures which lapped up whatever treatment was on offer at surface level. This of course meant that the soil element of Burgundian terroir was having almost no influence at all on the grapes. According to one respected French soil scientist, Claude Bourguignon, many Côte d'Or vineyards at the start of the 1990s showed less microbial activity than the Sahara desert.

Vineyard applications: trick or treat?

Today, Claude, like most forward-thinking growers in Burgundy and indeed throughout the world, has moved away from the chemical treatments to a much more sympathetic approach to viticulture – some call it biodynamic, others organic. Certainly the fertilisers he uses are of organic origin, while weeds and cover crops between the rows are ploughed into the soil rather than being zapped with weedkiller. Tractors are used as infrequently as possible so the soil doesn't become compacted, and thus impenetrable to the vines' roots. Some domaines even go to the extent of applying treatments by helicopter, and you'll see large, bright plastic bags attached to the ends of the vine rows to show the pilots exactly where they should be spraying their payload.

Better canopy management reduces the need for sprays against mildew and botrytis. Even so, a blue tinge to the vine leaves shows that Bordeaux mixture – a blend of copper sulphate, lime and water – is still widely used to control downy mildew. Birds are never as great a problem in Burgundy as in other parts of the wine world, but moths and insects can be, since they chew leaves and spread diseases. There are, of course, insecticides to control these, but Claude now has a new weapon in his anti-bug armoury: he hangs little white sachets containing pheromones throughout the vineyard, and as the wind blows through them their contents are released. The insects become confused sexually (and who hasn't been there?) and decide that there are probably better places to mate and lay their eggs.

Despite all Claude's efforts, his vines still succumb to predators and disease from time to time. The green sway of the vineyards is interrupted by patches of yellow, evidence of a viral infection which will reduce the yield and delay the ripening. There's very little that can be done about this invasion, apart from ripping the offending plants out and replanting with new, virus-free vines.

Getting down to work

From veraison to harvest, it's the vines that do most of the work in the vineyard. Claude finds time to move into a new house in Beaune, but is still on hand to deal with any problems that arise. The weather in the second half of August is patchy, and a hailstorm has hit a portion of the Marsannay vineyard. It looks more than anything as if someone has been through chewing the leaves and slashing at the grapes. The damaged bunches are at risk of fungal infection and need to be cut off, but Claude is reasonably happy that this is the worst of his problems.

Above and below. The barber and the customer. *These rows of vines catching the midday sun in late August would benefit from a haircut so the grapes can enjoy a last fling in the summer sun*

The vineyards, though mostly empty, aren't necessarily quiet. The hordes of fat-bottomed cyclists who descend on Burgundy each summer in ill-considered lycra are often shocked out of their saddles by the sound of what appears to be gunshot. Birds love grapes, and although they don't wreak the havoc here that they do in other vineyard regions, they are still a nuisance. Automated bird-scarers, which explode loudly at regular intervals, help reduce the risk, and also give the locals a giggle at the tourists' expense.

Looking good for harvest

This and the small amount of hail damage apart, the end of August sees Claude in optimistic mood for the vintage. This has been a good year, with hardly any problems in the vineyards, and the growing season is probably a week ahead of the norm. There was some quite heavy rain in July – which caused problems with mildew – but this came before veraison, at a time when the vines weren't at risk of infection.

The rain also topped up the underground water supplies, so even in the heat of August the vines didn't suffer from water stress. Lack of water can be a problem in hot, dry vintages, as the vines' resources are diverted into reducing moisture loss rather than ripening the fruit. The Burgundians are forbidden by AOC law from irrigating their vines, but there are many who feel that there should be special dispensation in tricky vintages. There are also the sneaky ones, who at such times are seen in the vineyard at strange hours applying a special spray consisting of two parts of hydrogen to every one part of oxygen.

Such measures have not been necessary in 2000. Apart from the odd storm or two, the sun has shone and the rain has fallen at the right times. Inside the grapes the sugar level is rising and the acid level falling. Claude takes some grape samples back to the winery lab so that the team can predict roughly when the harvest should begin in each vineyard. Sugar level can be determined with a special piece of equipment called a refractometer, but as we saw earlier, this only constitutes one element of ripeness. There's nothing at present which can determine phenolic ripeness better than tasting the grapes. So as August turns to September, Claude, Jacques, Christine and Pierre-Henry can be found outside the winery chewing and spitting out pips. Primitive maybe, but remarkably effective.

LA BAUME

SUGAR, SUGAR

'After some recent vintages, I'm thinking of throwing away my refractometer,' says Ashley. 'We're much less concerned with the sugar levels now than with obtaining physiological ripeness. Sure, the grapes need to have a certain potential alcohol, but once they've achieved that, then the decision as to when to pick is based purely on taste. There's no such thing as a typical year here, and once again, the best illustration is the 1998 and 1999 vintages. In 1998, our Sélection Chardonnay had 14.5% alcohol. In 1999, it had 12.5%. Everyone we've ever shown them to has thought they were very similar in style, and has been astonished at this difference.'

the harvest

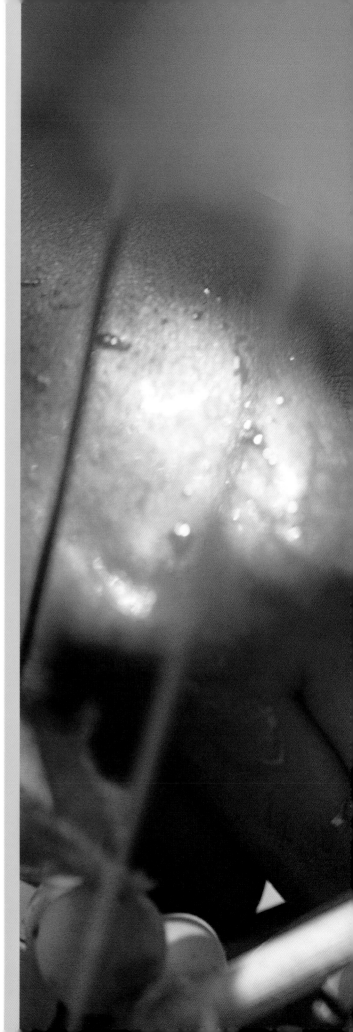

'The harvest is a stimulating and frenetic time, packed with excitement and expectation. Turning grapes into memorable wine requires good knowledge of the vineyard and grape quality, picking at optimum ripeness, a well-prepared winery and cellar team, and a lot of luck with the weather.'

DAVID BAVERSTOCK,
PORTUGUESE WINEMAKER

Visit Burgundy in September and you risk treading in something soft and squelchy in the street. But it's no reason to curse the local canine population: chances are you've stepped on a bunch of grapes that's fallen from a truck. They're everywhere. This is harvest time; the busiest, noisiest, most chaotic and most crucial time in the wine calendar. The streets are sticky with grape juice, there's a heady aroma on the breeze, and even those not directly involved in the wine business find themselves swept up in the buoyant atmosphere.

Above. Man vs Machine.
While a refractometer is useful for measuring sugar levels, the best way of determining when to pick is to taste the grapes

'Even today in many parts of Europe, you'll find wineries around which a vinegar-like stench obstinately settles, and the owners don't even seem to notice – let alone care.'

For 11 months of the year, the fermentation hall at La Sablière, Jadot's Beaune winery, is as quiet as a local library and could almost pass for a building of religious significance, a feeling enhanced by the unusual design of the place. Under a soaring chestnut roof, which would grace a cathedral, there are four concentric circles of fermentation vats – stainless steel for the outer two, wood for the inner two – and the grapes can be pumped into any of these through a central pipe with rotating hydraulic limbs. Beneath the pipe is a raised wooden platform on which the high priest of this temple, Jacques Lardière, is holding forth.

'Normally there is nothing happening here. We might store a little wine in the steel tanks, but that's about it. It's very lovely, *hein*? Of course we designed it to be easy to use and easy to maintain, but I also believe that the circular form gives it, gives it...' His large hands begin to rotate at spin-dryer speed. 'It harnesses the vibrations in the soils; it focuses their energy...' A pause for thought. 'It excites the macromolecules; it means that the macromolecules which are in the soil of each vineyard get a chance to speak in the wine. You understand?' Er, yes Jacques, of course.

Cleaning up the act
The peace is about to be shattered, but first of all there are a few vital tasks to be performed. All the winemaking equipment which will be pressed into use in the coming weeks must first be located, checked and serviced. It also has to be thoroughly cleaned.

Only over the last decade has the importance of hygiene troubled most producers in traditional European regions. Indeed, many of the flavours in certain wines which had been attributed to the local terroir can now be traced back to dirty cellars.

Anthony Hanson, in his seminal book on burgundy, says: 'In Burgundy, it used to be quite common to celebrate the earthy, gamey elemental aromas which were present, and they were often thought to be linked to the wine's geographical origin. We did not realise the extent to which a smell recalling chickens' innards, for instance, might be more due to microbial activity in the lees of the barrel than the subtle mixture of marls, clays, pebbles and limestone on the vineyard slope', (*Burgundy*, Faber & Faber, 2nd edition, 1995).

In modern wineries, where a great deal of the equipment is made from stainless steel, the task of keeping everything clean is fairly straightforward, even if conservationists might raise their eyebrows at the gallons and gallons of water that are used each day. Many older cellars, however, were not planned with hygiene in mind. Here, wooden rather than steel vats are the norm, and the upkeep of these is considerably more laborious. Mould growing on the walls isn't a sign of shoddy maintenance, and indeed in some parts of the world, notably Tokaji in Hungary, this is often encouraged, as the producers feel that it contributes to the character of the wine. But the bad cellars are very easy to spot – all you have to do is simply follow your nose. Today,

Above. Less bovva wiv' a hovva.
A daredevil chopper pilot gives the vineyards a quick blow dry

across Europe, you'll still find wineries around which a vinegar-like stench obstinately settles, and the owners don't even seem to notice – let alone care.

Shifting it all around

But with the arrival of the first grapes only days away, La Sablière looks and smells as clean as a hospital. In an upper room overlooking the 83 vats, Jacques, Pierre-Henry and Christine are huddled around a computer screen planning their campaign for the next few weeks. Even for those producers who make only half a dozen different wines, this is something of a logistical challenge. For a winery that will be processing literally hundreds of different batches of grapes, it can be a nightmare.

Each vintage brings its own challenges. The 2000 growing season has been very good, with only the Marsannay vines giving cause for concern, so there will be no need to wait nervously for certain vineyards to finish ripening. However, the volumes look set to be larger than usual. It's a nice problem to have, but it's still a problem. Where is it all going to go? That batch of Beaune premier cru which fitted into a small tank last year will certainly need a larger vessel this time around.

The three of them are reasonably confident as to how the vintage will progress in Jadot's vineyards, but they are also to some degree at the mercy of the growers who sell Jadot grapes and grape juice. The lorries bringing these don't always arrive when they're supposed to, and in a year like this, their cargo may be significantly larger than expected. Even if it isn't, there's still concern as to whether there will be enough space for all the wine. Eventually, they formulate a schedule which they believe will work. If it rains, they'll have to rethink, but for the moment they're happy.

Claude isn't. He too is gearing up for vintage, and today is the day for checking that he has enough secateurs, gloves, picking boxes, and other harvest paraphernalia. He has just arrived at the shed where these are stored to discover one of the vine-straddling tractors lying on its side looking decidedly the worse for wear. (Since the rows in Burgundian vineyards are so close together, there's no way a conventional tractor could navigate through the vineyard. This has led to some ingenious engineering from tractor manufacturers – vehicles which span one and occasionally two rows of vines, and which can be adapted to

perform any number of tasks from pruning to leaf-plucking to picking.) This particular tractor isn't especially new, and it's not absolutely essential for the forthcoming harvest, but Claude is still concerned for its welfare. His only comfort is that it can't have been in that state for too long. Just the previous week it was being used for 'hedging' the vines – giving them a final trim in order to expose the grapes to the last few rays of sun. It's not a crucial task, but it does give a final boost to the physiological ripeness of the fruit. Hedging also makes it easier for the pickers to get at the bunches of grapes.

It'll be alright on the night...

Claude has been keeping a close eye on the vineyards in Marsannay which were affected by hail. Some of the grapes which were damaged and split in the storm have fallen to the ground, but many still cling to the bunches, and there are several instances of rot. It's too late in the season to apply any chemical sprays, as they could not only affect the flavour of the wine, but also inhibit the working of the natural yeasts during fermentation. He and his men have been through and snipped off the worst bunches, but he

Below. Along for the ride. *Even though they aren't to everyone's liking, mechanical harvesters are becoming more and more common on the Côte d'Or*

has his fingers crossed for good weather until harvest. This may bring the remaining fruit to full maturity, although since the leaves are damaged, there's a strong likelihood that the ripening process will be inhibited.

The secateurs all seem to be in good working order, but Claude is concerned as to whether he'll have enough people to wield them in this larger-than-average vintage. In Burgundy, as in many European wine regions, it is becoming increasingly difficult to find any grape pickers – never mind experienced ones – at harvest time. With not long to go until the *ban des vendanges* – the official starting date for the harvest determined by the appellation contrôlée authorities – he's going to have to spend a few hours on the phone trying to muster up more bodies for the two teams of pickers which Jadot puts to work on the Côte d'Or.

Dissent in the ranks

A sunny morning in mid-September, and Claude is still not happy. Vintage began a week earlier and he had hoped that, by now, with the halfway stage in sight, his 40-strong team which is picking the Côte de Beaune vineyards wouldn't need quite so much husbanding. It's an odd mix of people, several of whom have been bussed in from the town of Le Creusot about 50 kilometres away to the southwest. A few have been doing the vintage with Jadot for some years, often alongside other members of their family. For many, however, this is their first time working in a vineyard

LA BAUME

CRISIS? WHAT CRISIS

There may be a general shortage of skilled grape pickers in French vineyards, but it doesn't have much of an effect on La Baume. 'I know some of my neighbours can't find enough pickers, but my only concern is whether I have enough fuel for the mechanical harvesters.' Ashley takes in grapes from 500 or so hectares of vineyards each vintage, and 499 of these are picked by machine. 'There's just one hectare that isn't and that can't be mechanised because of the soil. Half way up the rows, the flavour profile of the fruit changes, so we pick it at two different times. You can't do that with a machine. Once it's set off up a row, that's it!'

Right. Crush on you. *The equipment at many small domaines may be rudimentary, but the wine could very well be fabulous. Here, grapes are being tipped into a well-used crusher*

and they've had to learn from scratch how to wield a pair of secateurs. Most are under 30.

The most vocal are a group of young Algerians who are anxious to pose for the camera with broad smiles, bandanas and V-signs. 'You live in Manchester? Ah, Manchester United: you have Barthez, the best goalkeeper in the world! *Vive le football*, it is the universal language'. They then point to a dreadlocked woman a few vine rows away who is doing her level best to conceal her contempt. 'Voici Rita Marley!'

Away from their peers, the perma-grins slip. '*C'est dur*', says Lahdi, a handsome, wiry 19-year-old. 'It's tough. Today, everyone wants to live in the cities, and it's becoming more and more difficult to find decent work in the countryside. I'm a trained carpenter, but I still have to do this in order to make a living'.

If some of Lahdi's chums don't buck up, they won't be making a living at all. Two of them have stopped for a cigarette which smells as if it might be packed with more than just tobacco, and Claude has to give them a strong verbal prod to get back to work. He sighs. 'This is a bad team. With a good group of pickers, everyone moves at roughly the same pace. But here, the quick ones are moving twice as fast as the slow ones. Ideally, you have people you know, but nowadays that's just not possible'.

Holidaying on the Côtes

The situation is much the same for Claude's colleague Jerry, who is in charge of a larger group of pickers operating in other vineyards in the Côte de Nuits. Most of that team is based in Dijon, just north of Marsannay, and while Jerry is on first-name terms with more than half the pickers, there are fewer and fewer familiar faces each year.

Meanwhile, in the Côte de Beaune the workers' banter seems to have ceased for a moment, and from a distance, all that can be seen of the harvesters is their bent backs and the occasional pall of cigarette smoke. First to the end of the row is Christine. So what are the secrets of grape picking for this *vendangeuse à grande vitesse*? 'Keeping quiet and keeping going.' This is her third harvest; prior to that she was at school. 'Now I've got two children to bring up, so this is something of a holiday for me.' It's a paid holiday too, although no-one is going to get rich on the wages of FF300 (£30) a day.

It's also a holiday for Christian, a nurse from Annecy in the Savoie. 'I grew up in the countryside in Brittany, and I always like to do the vintage as it's a way of keeping in touch with the land.' While he's been coming to Burgundy for several years now, leaving his wife and children at home for the fortnight of the vintage, he's not sure whether he'll be returning in the future. 'It used to be a festival, with everyone working together, living together, eating together and sleeping together. Now there's just not the same atmosphere, not the same camaraderie.'

One solution to the problem of disappearing pickers can be seen a few vineyards further up the hill, right among the vines. It's a

LA BAUME

WHEN I SAY PICK, PICK
La Baume takes in fruit from 35 different growers scattered around the Languedoc. However, the decision as to when to pick is entirely down to Ashley and his team. 'We can specify the time they start the harvest down to the hour. The growers have to do the actual picking, but we make sure that they can get hold of a machine as and when they need it. There are businesses here now which can hire out the right equipment, or if one of our harvesters is free, they can use that.'

Above and right. Exhibits A, B, C...
*Turning grapes into wine requires
a veritable cornucopia of widgets,
thingamajigs and spongy orange balls*

mechanical harvester, a machine which can pick more fruit in an eight-hour day than one man could harvest in a fortnight. These picking machines straddle the vine rows, slapping the plants with finger-like rods. This shakes the grapes onto a conveyor belt below, which then carries them off into a hopper. They're becoming more and more common in the region, and it isn't to everyone's liking. 'It is so brutal', says Jacques, shaking his head. 'They wreck the vineyards and they wreck the fruit too. I would like to see them banned in the Côte d'Or, and certainly from the grands and premiers crus.'

Man and machine – imperfect harmony
Watching this particular machine and its three-man crew, you can understand his concern. The driver is threading his way up and down a steep site at the top of a slope that was not planted with mechanisation in mind. Turning the machine round in the tiny gap at the end of each row requires consummate skill, and copious instructions from the two men seated on the back, and every now and then the harvester takes a small section of a wall with it, or triggers a mini-landslide.

Not so far away, a much more modern machine is at work. Whereas the older harvesters have metal rods which strike the branches of the vine, this one has fibreglass ones which hit the foliage and appear to do much less damage. The vineyard is also better suited to mechanisation, being slightly flatter and having more space to manoeuvre. A quick look at the grapes gathered in

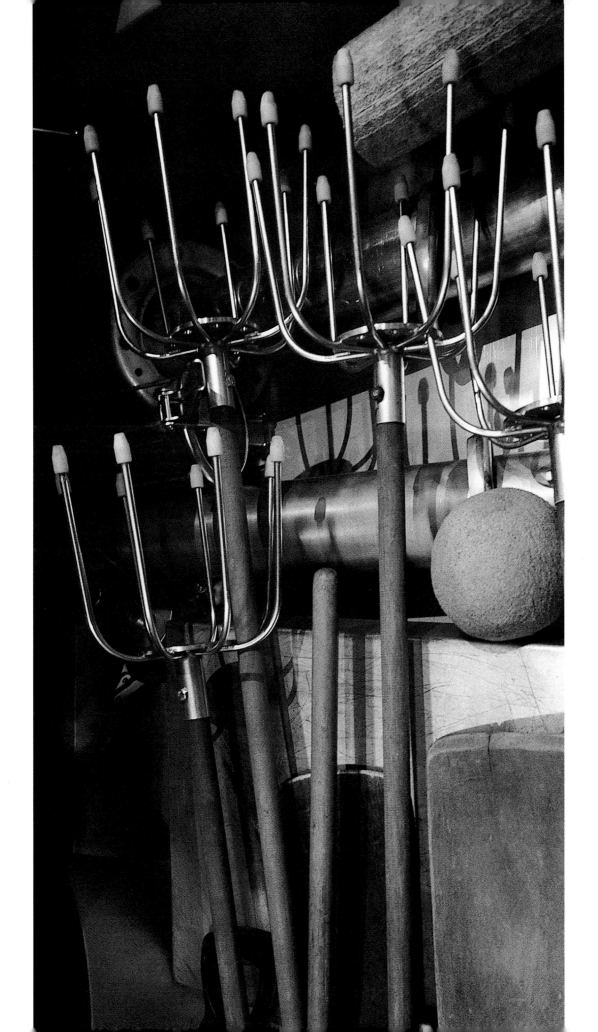

Above. Tanked up. *Stainless steel tanks, some of them stacked two or three high, are checked and cleaned prior to being filled with white grape juice*

the hopper reveals healthier fruit and far less MOG – Matter Other than Grapes, as the Aussies call it – than with the more primitive machines. Its owner was more than happy with the results he obtained last year, the first time he used the mechanical harvester, although he still can't quite believe that this machine can do the job of 20 pickers in a fraction of the time.

'In 1999, I used it mainly for reds. The whites were all picked by hand apart from one vineyard which I thought I'd try harvesting with the mechanical harvester. Many people told me that the machine bashed the white grapes around too much, but I'm happy with the way the wine has turned out. So this year, the only white vineyards I'm doing by hand are the grands crus, and if I have no problems, then I may even use the machine for them next time. No, it is not pretty, but it is efficient, and will pay for itself in a few years.'

Archaic machine harvesters aren't the only things which destroy walls. A van has pulled up on the lane close to where Claude's team is working, and a human chain is formed to transfer its contents – stacks of green and blue plastic boxes embossed with the Louis Jadot name – into the vineyards. One of the links is too energetic and doesn't aim straight, hurling the boxes into a rather lovely crumbling limestone wall, dislodging several stones in the process. Claude tuts.

The porters pile the boxes up on their barrows and wheel them up and down the rows to the pickers. One of them, a prime candidate for the Monsieur Muscley Calves of Burgundy award, manages to keep a yellowing cigarette balanced in his mouth throughout the whole process. When they've unloaded all the empty crates, they then gather up the full ones and take these back to be stacked up in the van. The plastic boxes into which the grapes are picked may not have the rustic air of the traditional wicker back-baskets but, being shallow, they are much kinder to the grapes. They're also a lot easier to keep clean.

Lunchtime, and the living is easy

There's not much being dropped into the baskets right now. Claude had been hoping to finish picking this vineyard before midday, but it just wasn't going to happen. Bending over vines since 8am has given the pickers a hearty appetite, so the secateurs are downed, the sticky gloves are removed and it's out with the lunchboxes. It's baking hot, so everyone is seeking shelter from the sun. Some pickers are huddled against walls, others sit in a group beneath a tree, while others are content to lounge in the shade under the vines.

Paolo is perspiring heavily, which is no surprise since he's been wearing a multi-coloured cagoule all morning. Beneath is a blue shirt with the world's largest sweat patch, which covers his entire back and extends under his armpits into an archipelago-like formation on his chest. Originally from northern Italy, this jovial moustachioed barrel of a man has lived in France for nearly half his life. 'I came here on holiday 30 years ago and never left. Where are you from in England? Ah, Manchester? I am Eric Cantona in disguise. I will give you a song.' He does. '*En Angleterre, en Angleterre, ils baisent par terre!*' It's not to be repeated in polite company, and the critical appraisal it receives includes a volley of orange peel and chunks of baguette.

Françoise shows me a large dish of pasta which, like the lady herself, is round, well-filled and smelling of meat. '*Mangez, mangez,*

LA BAUME

I'M GONNA WAIT TILL THE MIDNIGHT HOUR

Providing there's someone to drive them, the mechanical harvesters can pick 24 hours a day. Where white grapes are concerned, however, there's only a small part of each day that is suitable. 'The way I always explain it,' says Ashley, 'is with apples. It's summer, the middle of the day, you've just peeled an apple and then the phone goes. You come back ten minutes later, and the apple's gone brown. But if it's midnight and the same thing happens, then your apple's pretty much the same. The high temperature of the day just makes the fruit oxidise more, and I don't want that.' The upshot is that picking of white grapes begins at midnight and runs through till around 5am.

mangez', she exhorts. It's good, even if it is enough to feed a hungry foursome. Is this what she eats every day? '*Non, mais j'en ai marre de casse-croûte*.' (No, but I'm sick of snack food.)

Not far away, there's a van rocking from side to side. Is there something going on inside which shouldn't be, two people carried away by the madness of vintage? No, it's Madame Deschamps, who is struggling to pull a large gas barbecue through the rear doors. Eventually she manages, only to discover that she's left one of the *grilles* at home. Never mind, she thinks she can improvise. Then she's back in the van for oven gloves, skewers and a large pair of tongs. These are followed by the feast: bread, a cool-box full of salad, no fewer than four different types of sausage, and plenty more to eat. She hastily says, 'It's not all for me, honestly. I'm cooking for my husband and two friends as well.' The barbie is fired up and soon the smell of sizzling sausages fills the air, attracting envious looks from those who are dining on cheese sandwiches and an apple.

Françoise has made a valiant attempt to finish her lunch, but there was too much even for her. Now she's propped up against a wall, half asleep with her head lolling from side to side. Those with more energy are kicking a football about, although with little conviction. They've been working under the blazing sun all morning, and while there is now the odd cloud in the sky, it's still too hot to run around.

Vine to van to vat

At 1.15 it's back to work, and half an hour later all the grapes have been picked. With the boxes stacked up and secured, the van sets off for the winery, five minutes' drive away. It's not the

first to arrive at La Sablière that day, and, all going to plan, it certainly won't be the last.

Upstairs in the office, Christine is on the phone. Another phone, held together with yellowing sticky tape, chirrups in her back pocket. Like a blonde vulture, she somehow manages to hunch up her shoulders and balance a phone against each ear while scribbling furiously. Eventually the shoulders drop, and she's quiet for a moment. How much sleep is she getting? A shrug and a curl of the bottom lip indicate that at times like this, eight hours' kip is not a serious option. She, and Jacques too, got to bed at 2.30am this morning, and both were back in the winery at 8am, a pace that they'll maintain throughout the 15 or so days of vintage. There's a slightly mad glint in their eyes.

Outside, the normally quiet courtyard is a hive of activity. In one corner a green-and-white striped tent has been erected. Beneath it, several stacks of grapes are sheltering, waiting to be processed. By the entrance to the winery, about a dozen people are clustered around two mini conveyor belts. A tanker stands nearby, and there's a lorry and a van humming away, waiting to be unloaded.

Philippe is the gruff and portly master of the courtyard. From his vantage point in the driving seat of one of the two fork-lift trucks, he can keep an eye on all the workers, as well as on any vehicles which come through either of the two gates. He is a man who elevates the art of fork-lift truck driving to the levels of Schumacher and Hakkinen. Careering around the yard at a

'"Ah, you are back with your camera and your notebook – you are from the tax department? Or the police?" A shout comes from nearby, "Ils sont Starsky et Hutch!"'

frightening pace, he beeps and swears furiously at anybody who gets in his way. One of the poles supporting the tent bears the scars of a close encounter of the fork-lift kind, and several pallets have also seen better days.

The lorry is bringing new barrels from Tonnellerie Cadus, the cooperage in which Jadot has a 35 per cent share. With these, Philippe is as gentle as a lamb, and they reach the ground unharmed. From here, the barrel-hand rolls them off towards the lift down to the cellar, with a dexterity born of much practice. What's the secret? 'It's like driving a cow', he says. 'If you start it off in the right direction and take it easy, it will stick to the path – usually.'

Rain spoils play

The van contains the crates of grapes which Claude's team picked earlier. It's being driven by Monsieur Deschamps, who is still wearing a smile from his lunchtime feast in the vineyard. His smile droops almost as much as his moustache when the rear doors are unlocked: one of the boxes has worked its way loose on the short journey and its contents have spilled out onto the floor of the van. With the opening of the door, many grapes tumble onto the ground. Philippe responds with a few seconds of colourful expletives, after which he tells one of his minions to throw the grapes in the nearest bin. The mess is eventually cleared up, and he is finally able to remove the rest of the crates, which are stacked up on palates in the van, to their lodgings under the tent. So far today, the tent has been needed to shade the fruit from the sun, but the clouds have been gathering since lunchtime and there are even a few spots of rain in the air.

The tanker is full of grape juice from a grower in St-Romain. Although the Jadot domaines are large, they don't supply enough fruit for the company's increasing requirements. One of Jacques Lardière's tasks in the 11 months of the year when he does go to bed at a reasonable hour is to seek out dependable growers throughout Burgundy who will be able to supply grapes or juice come vintage time. Some of these have been dealing with Jadot for decades, while others will be delivering to La Sablière for the first time in 2000.

St-Romain may not be the greatest white-wine appellation in the Côte d'Or, but Jacques has been dealing with this supplier for several years and trusts him. Certainly the juice which is being

Above. Click, click go the shears. *Harvesting can be backbreaking work. The grapes are picked into these small buckets which are then tipped into larger stackable plastic trays*

Above. All present and correct.
While Claude doesn't call out the register each morning, he needs to know how many pickers he has in order to plan each day – and to make sure that no one is overpaid at the end of the week

pumped into a tank in the winery tastes delicious. Not all of it ends up in the tank. The last few litres are put into one of the older barrels from the cellar, and as the driver leaves, this has pride of place next to him on the passenger seat – with a seat belt on, of course.

Philippe has emptied Monsieur Deschamps' van and is now loading it up with empty crates. With the rain falling more heavily, it's not the most pleasant of tasks, and his grimace becomes grimmer. In the vineyards, the conditions are also affecting the pickers. Those wearing sun hats are slightly drier than the others, but the general atmosphere is damper than the weather. At 4.15, an hour earlier than normal and with more than half of the vineyard still unpicked, Claude decides to call it a day. The pickers traipse back to their bus worn out and soggy, and even the cocky youngsters can only muster a weary grin. 'Bye-bye Manchester. See you tomorrow.'

Despite the early finish, Claude's not too despondent. 'They were a bit slow this morning, those guys, but they've had a good day. We've done as much as I'd hoped to do, even with the lost hour.' He also has high hopes for the vintage as a whole. 'It's a good year. We had some rain about ten days before we started picking, which was just what the vines needed, and all the grapes are looking remarkably healthy.' He points out some bunches of white grapes which got slightly burned by the sun during the August heat. Their skins are noticeably brown, and their flavour is much sweeter than the unaffected grapes, like cooked apples in fact. 'I like the flavour, and it can be beneficial to the wine, providing there's not too much of it.'

'Plan B' into action

Claude himself still has work to do – the rain means that the picking schedule needs altering. The plan had been to pick one of the premier cru sites in Beaune the following morning, but he's reluctant to do this because further rain could cause the grapes to swell up and thus dilute their flavours. If that does happen, he'd prefer to wait for finer weather, by which time the fruit will have dried out and shrunk back to normal size. He'll have to pick something of a lower quality level instead, but before deciding which site to go for, he'll need a chat with Pierre-Henry Gagey and Jacques.

Above. Sticky fingers. *The Marigolds keep some of the grape juice off the pickers' hands, but even so, the end of the day sees everyone calling for strong soap and scrubbing brushes – or a cat...*

Pierre-Henry is getting slightly more sleep than Jacques, but is still working 12 hours or more most days. 'It's a nightmare at the moment', he sighs. 'We have a lot of grapes to get through, and I'm actually glad that the rain stopped the pickers. It means that there won't be so much work to do tonight.'

Picked one? Nice one, get sorting

He and Jacques are currently doing duty on the mini conveyor belts – or sorting tables, to give them their proper name. A crate of grapes is tipped out at one end, and as the fruit travels up the table, five pairs of hands sort through it, removing any leaves and looking for any unhealthy bunches of grapes which the pickers haven't spotted. Some bunches can be salvaged with a judicious snip of the secateurs, but most of them are discarded and end up in a skip at the far end of the courtyard, which is now buzzing with fruit flies.

Several of those manning the tables are students from the oenological college in nearby Dijon. For most, it's their first time working in a winery. Their job may appear less tiring than that of the pickers and although it requires just as much concentration, it's also very monotonous, and it's no surprise that the occasional mouldy bunch, and even the odd caterpillar or two, makes its way to the end of the table and into the destemmer. When there are no grapes to sort, they spend their time cleaning the grape boxes, and only when they've finished this to Philippe's satisfaction do they get the chance to sit down for a well-earned cigarette.

Sizing up the workload

There are two six-hour shifts each day: 9.30am to 3.30pm, and 3.30pm to 9.30pm. At least that's what the rota pinned up on the office wall says. In practice, the second shift finishes when there are no more grapes to process. Surveying the stacks of crates under the tent, Kim, who has come from Korea to study at Dijon, reckons that there are three hours' work still to do, which would mean finishing at 10pm. The previous night they knocked off after midnight.

With the arrival of the next batch of fruit, Pierre-Henry and Jacques take an even keener interest in the sorting tables. These grapes come from the hail-affected section of Marsannay. The pair of them visited the vineyard a few days earlier to assess the damage to the vines, and taste the grapes, and ideally would have liked to have waited a few more days before picking them. However, the morning weather forecast had predicted rain for the afternoon, and in order to prevent further damage to the fruit, they took the decision to harvest today.

LA BAUME

QUEST FOR QUALITY
Ashley makes no apologies for his mechanical harvesters. 'People think that machine-harvested fruit is inferior, but providing it's a modern machine with a good driver, I don't believe it is. Whites are certainly more problematic than reds. We harvest everything into small bins, so the grapes don't get crushed, and then aim to get the fruit to the winery as quickly as possible. Some vineyards are five minutes away, others are three hours away. But because we use small bins and night picking, everything reaches here in good condition.'

From a distance, the grapes look exactly the same as those from any other vineyard. However, on closer inspection the rot is all too plain to see, even though the pickers have left the worst bunches in the vineyard. The sorters are soon at work with their secateurs, cutting out the rotten grapes as well as they can and saving as much of the rest of the bunch as possible. Jacques tastes the grapes, and his expression isn't a happy one. But nor is it a frown. 'I don't know. It's not ideal, and we will have to keep our eye on how the wine develops. But it could be far, far worse.'

Guillaume de Castellane arrives and its time for the three of them to go into the lab to taste some wine. Guillaume is in charge of Château des Jacques, the Moulin-à-Vent estate which Jadot bought in 1997, and he's brought along some early samples from the 2000 vintage for the team to assess.

A new Beaujolais on the table

The wines which Jadot has been producing there have caused something of a stir, since they have a great deal more *matière* – more substance – than is really typical of beaujolais wine. Moulin-à-Vent is one of the top ten villages to be found in Beaujolais, and in general makes sturdier wine than is the norm for the region. However, the Château des Jacques wines, which include five clos (single-vineyard) cuvées, are full-bodied even for Moulin-à-Vent.

Above and left. The Lunch Bunch.
The most important time of the day for the pickers is their midday break. The food may vary but the enthusiasm with which it is consumed remains the same

Above. Shh, we're eating. *A perfect day, and the only sound is the clatter of cutlery*

Below. Merde, I forgot the mustard.

The line-up on the bench is of a dozen batches of wine, some of which have still not finished their fermentation. First up are a selection of whites. The top white wine from Château des Jacques is a single-vineyard wine called Clos de Loyse. 'It's a nice wine', says Jacques, 'but at the moment it is not remarkable. Maybe in three years, we will have something to talk about, something which is original.' A quick pause to taste one of the cuvées. 'At the moment, Clos de Loyse is only a bourgogne blanc. We'd rather make a good bourgogne blanc than a so-so beaujolais, or indeed any other appellation. That is the problem in parts of Burgundy now, especially for those in the Mâconnais. If producers of mâcon blanc are to survive, they need to make something which can't be made elsewhere.'

Then come the reds. They're not the best cuvées of the vintage, but they're still very impressive, with power and flavour in abundance. 'We had dreadful problems with hail this year, with one vineyard being entirely wiped out, so I'm pleased to see the wines looking so good', says Guillaume. 'It's going to be a great year', and everyone agrees.

But are they typical beaujolais? Jacques lifts his hands skywards in the most Gallic of gestures. 'What is typical? Normally, beaujolais is thought of as light and frivolous, a pretty wine, but it hasn't always been like that. We treat Gamay at Château des Jacques just as we do Pinot Noir here. We even have a sorting table there, which as far as I know is unique for Beaujolais. Our aim is to produce great Moulin-à-Vent with depth, which can age for a few years, not just something simple. We are getting there. Ah, Claude, welcome, come and try these wines.' A glass is pressed into the hand of the rather soggy new arrival, and the merits of the various wines are discussed at length.

Finally, Claude manages to corner Jacques and Pierre-Henry, and the three of them sit down to discuss which vineyard sites should be picked tomorrow. The rain has now stopped and the forecast is looking favourable. However, they play safe and decide to pick one of their basic Savigny-lès-Beaune vineyards rather than something more precious. They also have a chance to assess their progress with the vintage so far. Half the harvest is in, and more than half of the tanks in the winery are full. At 9pm, Claude finally heads for home – but not before nearly being maimed by Philippe on his fork-lift truck.

Chopper squad

The following morning the bus from Le Creusot empties its contents in Savigny. This time, Paolo is not the only one sporting a cagoule, although his is still the most colourful. 'Ah, you are back with your camera and your notebook – you are from the tax department? Or the police?' A shout comes from nearby, *'Ils sont Starsky et Hutch!'*

It's not raining, but there's plenty of rain from the previous evening still clinging to the vines. As the leaves flick against the pickers, those without decent waterproofs get wetter and wetter, not to mention grumpier and grumpier. They're not, however, as sodden as the people working for estates where there was no Claude to do the hedging at the end of August. In some vineyards the exuberant foliage has become a miniature rain forest, and the harvesters there are soaked to the skin.

One means of dealing with the excess moisture can be seen and heard on the other side of Savigny. It's a helicopter belonging to the Hospices de Beaune. The Hospices is a charitable foundation which raises money by auctioning the wines from its vineyards on the third Sunday of November each year. The vineyards have been donated by various benefactors over the centuries and, as a result, the Hospices is one of the largest landowners in the Côte

MAD DOGS & AUSTRALIANS
'The locals are always very interested in what we're doing, especially when they wake up in the middle of the night and see a mechanical harvester going past their window. Sometimes they think we're a good thing for the region, sometimes a bad thing. When we set up here in 1990, we were the first foreign company in the area, and it took quite a time to build up relationships with local growers. But once they saw what we were doing, and tried the wines, they began to take a little more interest, and actually started coming to us to offer their fruit.'

LA BAUME

TANK YOU VERY MUCH
Prior to the arrival of the BRL Hardy team in 1990, the winery at Domaine de la Baume was, in estate agent-speak, 'offering potential for development'. In other words it was derelict. The new owners gutted the building, laying new floors and installing shiny new stainless steel tanks. 'It was very difficult for us to find all the equipment we needed,' says Ashley. 'At the time, I'm not even sure if any other winery in the region had a refrigeration system installed. But now they're everywhere, and I like to think that that's partly our doing.'

d'Or. Here's a photo-opportunity if ever there was one, and the Clio sets off at breakneck speed. However, progress is hampered both by the pot-holes and puddles which punctuate the single-track dirt roads wriggling through the Côte d'Or, and by the many cars, tractors, vans and other harvest paraphernalia scattered along their verges.

After a ten-minute pursuit, the car screeches to a halt just as the helicopter flies off north. The word *merde* springs to mind. However, the pilot slows down about a kilometre away, so the chase is on again, and this time proves successful. The pilot is hovering with death-defying skill less than a metre above the section of the famous Corton-Charlemagne vineyard which belongs to the Hospices. He then moves a few rows further up the hillside and settles again. The idea is that the downdraught blows the water from the vines, enabling them to be picked in near-normal conditions. It's effective, but it could be the most expensive hairdryer in the world.

Only a few producers go to such trouble. Most just can't afford to, and even those who can aren't totally convinced of its efficacy. Jacques thinks that it's a good system for getting rid of the water, but Guillaume de Castellane disagrees: 'It's not the water on the grapes that is the problem, it's what gets into the grapes through their roots. If the water's just on the grapes, you pick them and it runs off. Or you can have driers set up on the side of the sorting tables.'

Rallying the troops

Claude's team is certainly managing without the benefit of a helicopter. The grumpiness slowly dissipates as the day brightens up, and vanishes as the morning break approaches. Several take advantage of the halt in proceedings to have, in the words of Winnie the Pooh, 'a little something' from the plastic vat in the back of Eric's van. It's a rough and ready red wine of dubious origin, and the ambient temperature only serves to accentuate its hard edges. This doesn't stop some of the pickers downing two, even three, plastic beakers of the stuff, with a chomp on a baguette to mop it up. Claude and his close friends, meanwhile, have a rather civilised interlude, featuring pâté, cheese, *jambon persillé, pain de campagne* and a glass of Jadot Mâcon Blanc Villages 1995 – slightly past its best, but still tasty.

Jean sits apart from the rest of the pickers, smoking quietly. Some of them think he's a trifle simple, but he just prefers to keep himself to himself. Claude likes him, however, and can often tell which rows he's been working on because of how thoroughly they've been picked. Jean also has a secret which he's not sharing with many people. 'You see my hands? Look at them. Why do you think they are cleaner than everyone else's? I tell you. It is my cat. Every evening, she comes and she licks them. It is the only way to get rid of all that grape juice.'

After the break, work is resumed in much better spirits, and the chatter level is high. There are those who can chatter while they

Below. Who nicked my back-pack?
Harvest is in full swing, and clutches of colourful figures are dotted around hillsides throughout the Côte d'Or

Above. Machine head. *Maybe there should be driving tests for the operators of machine harvesters. Certainly, a skilful driver can make a big difference to the quality of the fruit*

work, and those who can just chatter. Yet again, Claude has to raise his voice; this time to Saïd, who has just thrown a bunch of grapes at one of his mates. 'It was a rotten bunch', he protests, but Claude isn't impressed.

Leading the way up the rows today are Félix and his girlfriend Monique, the two who shared Madame Deschamps' barbecue. He's thin and serious with a closely shaven, rough-shaped head, while she's beautiful in a tousled, country sort of way. They talk quietly to each other throughout the day. After their stay in Burgundy they're planning to head off to the southwest, where they can get work pruning apple trees.

Is there an end in sight?

Their conversation is interrupted when a white van covered in muddy handprints and with bouquets of flowers jammed underneath its windscreen wipers screams past, horn blaring. From the half-open rear doors comes the sound of singing and raucous laughter, plus a white bottom, exposed for the benefit of anyone who cares to take a look. Someone has finished vintage. Is Claude close to finishing? He grins with his mouth but not his eyes. 'Non, non, non. We have another five days, maybe a week, to go.'

An hour later, the same van can be seen down a side street in Meursault. At least it looks like the same van, but then there are dozens of similar vehicles rushing round the Côte d'Or at this time of year, and the bosses of the van rental companies are all wearing broad grins. The arrival of this particular one has been observed by the patron of a restaurant in the square. It was difficult to miss, he said, since it drove round the square four times with the horn at full blast. Is it the end of the vintage for many in Meursault? 'It is the beginning of the end, at least.' He sighs, 'With all these machines they now use for the harvest, there are fewer celebrations like this each year. Vintage used to be two or three weeks, but now they do it in two or three days. It is a pity.'

The van now stands outside a pair of ornate iron gates leading into a small courtyard. Grapes picked that morning have been temporarily abandoned, and through an open door, the pickers can be seen enjoying their end-of-vintage lunch, a traditional *boeuf bourguignonne*. At this small domaine, the harvesters are all able to sit round one table. Most stay in the dormitory-style rooms above the press, which are there purely for the fortnight of the vintage. The men's room is on one side of the communal bathroom, the women's room on the other. Given the enthusiasm of their current celebrations, the boundaries between the two tonight could be, shall we say, somewhat flexible.

When they see that they have visitors, the revellers spill out into the courtyard. Their laughter is loud, their leering poorly concealed, and the air is thick with innuendo and the aroma of wine. Actually, the wine smells rather good, even from a rough tumbler. So it should, for it's a 1995 Clos de la Roche, a quantum leap from Eric's gut-rot red. It's being consumed with gusto rather than the reverence which some aficionados reserve for grand cru burgundy. And why shouldn't it be? If wine isn't all about

pleasure, then what IS it about? And it's not every day that the harvest comes to an end.

A neighbouring producer stops to observe the celebrations. He finished the day before, and after a day and night of revelry, his team of pickers has finally departed. 'I'm seriously thinking of using a machine for harvesting next year. The pickers are all very friendly, but my wife is getting sick of having them here each year. They expect her to cook for them, clean for them, wash for them, mend their clothes and more, even though they know she has a full-time job.' He sighs. 'Then there's all the bureaucracy. The workers used to just turn up and we'd pay them, but now you have to fill in this form, and that form, and when they cut themselves you have to fill in another form. It gets worse each year.'

Left and below. Yesssss! *Vintage is over at this domaine, but the celebrations are only just beginning*

Claude and his team have had a more sedate lunch. They finished their picking in Savigny at the end of the morning, and are all set for moving on to the Jadot section of Corton-Charlemagne for the afternoon shift. The weather has turned fine and sunny, and any excess moisture from the overnight rain has evaporated. It appears the helicopter wasn't necessary after all. With the last of the crates from Savigny loaded in the back of the van, Monsieur Deschamps makes sure that nothing will overbalance this time, and sets off to the winery – carefully.

Once again, his isn't the only vehicle making a delivery. The other large wagon has brought three stainless steel fermentation tanks, hired for the duration of this abundant vintage to cope with the surplus.

Just when you thought it was time to go home...

As Monsieur Deschamps pulls in, Jacques Lardière pulls out in his old blue Volvo with the well-worn leather seats. He's on his way to see a grower in the Hautes-Côtes, the name given to those vineyards in the upper, northwestern parts of the Côte d'Or. On the way, he finds time to phone his wife. 'Hello, it is your little Jacques calling, how are you today?' She doesn't see an awful lot of him at this time of year, nor of their daughter Mathilde, who has also been roped in to help at the winery.

Jacques makes a number of these trips each day to assess whether the grapes are ready to harvest. 'Normally, they struggle to get their fruit as ripe in the Hautes-Côtes as in the rest of the Côte d'Or, but in a warm vintage like this one, they can produce some very attractive wines.'

On arrival, he and the grower set off into the vineyard to do some analysis. Not with a refractometer though – Jacques doesn't possess one – because once again, it's the chomp and spit approach to testing grape ripeness. The verdict is 'Oui', so the grower starts ringing round to assemble his teams of harvesters, while Jacques heads off to another vineyard to repeat the procedure there.

Why not get a robot to do it?

When he gets back to the winery, it's 5.30pm, and the sorters are taking a well-earned break. Sorting tables are by no means common-place in Burgundy, and very few producers process enough grapes to justify having electrically powered ones, let alone two of them which are manned for more than 12 hours each day throughout the harvest. But the quality-conscious ones do make sure that they deal with only healthy grapes, and often do their sorting in the vineyard. The harvesters tip the grapes onto a temporary table mounted on the back of a trailer, and someone will watch over this, keeping the good grapes and throwing the bad ones into a heap on the ground, where they are left to rot away.

The two conveyor belts for the moment stand idle, and after a yawn and a stretch which reveals half his bottom, so too for a moment does Philippe. Only for a moment though. A van arrives carrying the fruit from Corton-Charlemagne which Claude and his team have just finished picking. There are some batches still under the tent waiting to be processed, but the grapes from this prestigious vineyard are deemed more important, so they jump to the front of the queue.

The sorting process isn't as critical for white grapes as for red, since their juice spends only the briefest of times in contact with the skins after crushing. Indeed, some batches are pumped straight into the press without being sorted. Jacques keeps an eye on the

Right. Here they come. *Grapes arrive at the winery on large trucks, small trucks and occasionally in cars*

Corton grapes as they travel up the table, but very little is picked out, even though some bunches seem to have elements of botrytis. 'Normally for reds, we would remove these, but for whites, a little bit of botrytis can bring an extra element to the wine.'

Time for business, but no suits round here mate

Jacques is called away from sorting duty by the arrival of one of his foreign importers, who is returning from holiday in southern France with his family. Wiping his hands on the black Levis which he has worn for most of the vintage, and which are now shiny and sticky with grape juice, he greets them with enthusiasm, and they set off for a quick tour round the winery.

Another recent arrival is Pierre-Henry, who, after a day in the office, is now back at the winery. Seeing his cellar master – the French have no word for 'winemaker' – disappearing into the distance, hands flapping as usual, he smiles. 'He is very good, Jacques, always enthusiastic, always passionate. When it comes to wine, he does not compromise. I want to find a way of giving him a bonus, but the taxes in France are so high. If I try to give him 100 francs, by the time it gets to him, the government has taken most of it, and he gets 23 francs.'

Having disposed of the importer, Jacques, Pierre-Henry, Christine and the recently arrived Claude gather in the lab for the evening progress report. The rain has delayed Claude slightly, but the pickers have had another good day, and Claude thinks that they will have

Opposite. Human chain. *These white grapes are being pumped straight into the press*

finished in four days, providing the weather holds. After a brief period of calculation, Christine reckons that, thanks to the three new tanks, they should just about have enough capacity in the winery for the rest of the vintage.

All that remains...

The Jadot team may not have finished picking, but the increasingly quiet vineyards are testimony that for many people, vintage is over. The white vans have been returned to the rental companies, while the pickers have gone back to their homes, many of them nursing hangovers. Some grapes can still be found on the vines, but only a few of these can be blamed on short-sighted harvesters. Most are what are known as shoulder bunches, a secondary crop of fruit which emerged only later in the season, long after the main crop had appeared. They're tart and mean, and leaving them on the vine is the best thing for them.

There are also the mounds of grapes on the vineyard floor, either from a tardy green harvest, or the cast-offs from the mobile sorting tables. If anyone had the inclination, they could probably sort through some of the latter and find enough unblemished berries to make a small amount of rather good wine. But the majority of the grapes have been transported back to the cellars. All that remains to be done is the minor task of turning them into wine.

LA BAUME

LIFE'S A BATCH

While the La Baume range runs to just 10 wines, Ashley receives dozens of separate batches of fruit every vintage, and handles each differently. With grapes arriving 24 hours a day, decisions as to how to treat each delivery have to be made on the hoof, and although he has another winemaker working alongside him, he doesn't see a great deal of his bed during vintage. (However, at least he is in full control of the place. A fellow Australian, working at another Languedoc winery, turned up early on a Saturday morning to check progress with the vintage, only to find that it had shut for the weekend. He was forced to climb over the gate and break in.)

red wine

'Red wine, like children, needs infinite attention and care after its birth to make it grow healthy and strong, and above all, to allow the character and personality to develop. The unique personality of truly great red wine is derived from a combination of grape variety, environment and man.'

PIERO ANTINORI, ITALIAN WINEMAKER

There are several schools and colleges around the world where you can go to learn the basics of winemaking. The worst graduates of these take the ground rules they have learned as a rigid recipe, and then proceed to make correct but soulless wines for the rest of their lives. The best students view their technical training as something much more flexible, something which is there to be accepted, ignored or moulded to fit. Great winemakers are usually great thinkers. But ask twelve of them for the best way to make Pinot Noir, and you will receive at least twelve different answers.

The first wine probably made itself, when an absent-minded farmer forgot about a batch of grapes he'd put in a bucket. Gradually the grapes at the bottom of the container were crushed under the weight of those above, and fermentation then began thanks to yeasts either on the grape skins or in the air. Returning to his bucket a week later, the farmer no doubt thought the fruit had been ruined, but then he tasted the liquid, and a smile came to his face. So if wine can make itself, what exactly does a winemaker do? Not a lot surely...

Ask Jacques Lardière what he as a winemaker does, and he will say, 'I'm not a winemaker, I'm a wine producer'. There is a difference. He describes himself not so much as a sculptor, expressing himself by chiselling something out of virgin rock, but as an educator entrusted with the task of nurturing and making the most of the raw material he is given so that it can express itself. This means that he has no formulaic approach to making, sorry, producing wine. What works with grapes from one vineyard will not necessarily be successful with those from another.

Stalk and stems, heroes or villains?

So what does Jacques as a wine producer do? A variety of things, really. On this particular September evening in Beaune, he is wheeling away the large bin full of grape stalks which stands near the sorting table and replacing it with an empty one. It may not be the best use of his expertise, but someone has to do it. The stalks have emerged from one end of a machine called a destemmer, into which the red grapes have travelled straight from the sorting table. It's a bit like a sieve with teeth on one side. The stalks poke through a grille and are grabbed by mechanical jaws, which pull and pull until all the grapes have dropped off.

Whether or not to destem is one of the many winemaking questions on which opinions differ. There was a time when the only means of destemming was by hand, and very few producers went to the trouble of doing so. But even now, with equipment which can do the task rapidly, some people still prefer to leave at least some of the stalks in with the grapes. The arguments from the anti-stalk brigade are that the stems contain bitter tannins which can leach out into the wine, and that they dilute the wine slightly, reducing its colour and alcoholic strength. The counter from the pro-stalk lobby is that the stems can give structure to a wine, and also that they help to break up the mass of grapes during maceration (see page 90).

That first crushing blow

The destemmer is actually a crusher-destemmer. The crushing part, which works by passing the grapes between two rotating rollers spaced far enough apart so they don't squash the seeds and release more astringent tannins, isn't being used at La Sablière. (Prior to such machines, treading by foot was the romantic but rather inefficient method of crushing.) Again, there are different schools

Opposite. Stalking heads. *Bunches go into one end of the destemmer, and this is what comes out of the other*

Left. Advice on tipping. *Jacques Lardière helps tip a bin of red grapes onto the sorting table, where several pairs of hands will check through for unhealthy fruit*

Opposite. Sorted. *The arrival of the grapes from the hail-affected vineyards in Marsannay calls for extra vigilance on the sorting table*

Left. Spot it and snip it. *Once it gets past the sorters, that's it. The eagle-eyed Christine is there to make sure that mistakes don't happen...*

of thought on the matter of crushing grapes. Crushing liberates the juice, and means that fermentation will be more predictable, starting (and thus finishing) earlier, and producing alcohol which will rapidly kill off any bacteria. However, as that first primitive winemaker discovered, crushing is not necessary since the grapes will eventually burst under their own weight in the fermentation vessel. In this respect, Jacques is primitive. Some grapes are split during destemming, but he prefers to leave the berries whole, as he feels that this adds extra character to the wine during fermentation.

Vat's all folks!

But before the grapes and their juice begin fermenting, they need something to ferment in. Fermentation vats for red wines come in all shapes and sizes, and in a wide variety of materials. Traditionally they were made from wood, usually oak. Some producers still prefer these, for aesthetic reasons as much as anything. In the first few years of use, they can add an oaky character to the wine, but after the fifth year they have little effect on the flavour. Cement vats lined with glass or epoxy resin are also widely found, especially in older wineries.

However, most modern wineries now use stainless steel tanks, usually with built-in cooling systems so that the fermentation temperature can be regulated. They have the added advantage of being easier to clean than wooden casks. La Sablière has a mixture

Above. Vat inclusive. *Wooden vats in the foreground and stainless steel vats in the background wait to be filled with red grapes*

CULTURE CLUB

Ashley's not one to beat about the bush. 'Natural yeast is a load of bollocks. Maybe it works where yeast cultures have built up over centuries, but if you've got a much shorter winemaking history, you're just playing with fire. Even if fermentation does start spontaneously, it often gives up when the wine's only got to 4% alcohol. We're still fascinated with the array of cultured yeasts available, and of course they never let you down, which is vital.'

of oak and steel vats in a variety of sizes ranging from less than 1,000 litres to more than 50,000 litres. The Jadot holdings in some vineyards such as Clos St-Denis and Musigny are so small that total production still doesn't fill one of the smallest vats.

Pumping up the vinous volume

The grapes are pumped from the destemmer to the vats. Pumping is very efficient – a modern pump can move as many grapes in an hour as a hundred men could do in a day – but it can be rather brutal. This is one reason why some producers of Pinot Noir, both in Burgundy and elsewhere, have designed their wineries on hillsides so that grapes and wine can be moved by gravity. Even so, using a decent pump to transport grapes through a wide pipe with few bends is no more brutal than putting them through a crusher. For a winery which has so many different *cuves* (vats) to deal with, pumping makes sense, and Jacques isn't too concerned that there will be any degradation in quality.

There's a batch of Chambolle-Musigny which has been along the sorting table and through the destemmer, and is now ready to be transferred to a vat. Before it's pumped in, the central pipe which feeds all the red fermentation vats needs to be cleaned out. The easiest way of doing this is by forcing a sterilised spongy ball the size of a large grapefruit through the hose. 'But', says Jacques, 'it is important that we put a small cage on the other end of pipe to catch the ball, otherwise – *poup, poup, poup* – it shoots out and flies around the winery.'

Once the pipe is totally clean, its hydraulic arm is rotated and extended to position the outlet above the vat. Then the pumping begins. The sound of the mass of grapes and juice emerging from the pipe is distinctive. Perhaps the politest way of describing it is to compare it with the noise you'd expect to come from a cow with a poorly tummy.

A few minutes later, the vat is full, though not according to the gauge on the outside because, as yet, very little juice has escaped from the grapes. For Jacques, this is one of the hallmarks of a good vintage. In the best years, the grapes are so ripe that they come off their stalks easily in the destemmer, and their skins are so thick that few have split by the time the fruit arrives in the vat.

Born to be wild

The ones which have split can now begin fermentation. Jacques is a firm believer in allowing wild yeasts, also known as native or indigenous yeasts, to start the fermentation. 'They are there, in the air, in the vineyards, on the grapes, in the winery, and they work. They are part of the terroir – why should I interfere with them?' He

Below. Stately pile. *A hillock of grapes straight out of the destemmer sits waiting to be pumped into a vat*

Above. Pressing matters. *A horizontal bladder press is given a final inspection before being filled with the mass of grapeskins and new wine*

feels that each of the many strains of yeast present adds another dimension to the wine. Some will be responsible for initiating fermentation, but will then be killed off when a certain amount of alcohol has been produced. Meanwhile, other yeast strains will take over the task, and then others again, until the job is finished. In his 30 years at Jadot, Jacques has never had a problem with a so-called stuck fermentation, in which a batch of wine has simply stopped fermenting before all the sugar has been converted into alcohol.

But not everyone has such confidence in wild yeasts. The point is that they are unpredictable, and for this reason, many producers use a single strain of a cultured yeast, which ensures that the fermentation will proceed smoothly. Burgundy has been making wine for centuries, during which time the yeast population has had a chance to expand and stabilise. However, in other regions with much shorter histories of wine production, there may be very little in the way of wild yeast, so it makes sense to use commercial strains. Certainly there are several fine wines made using cultured yeasts, even in Burgundy, not to mention dozens of dreadful ones where wild yeasts have had their way. Mention this to Jacques and he screws his mouth up in disgust. It is not the yeasts which are the problem, it is men interfering with them. Anyway, fermentations at La Sablière are allowed to proceed with the very minimum of intervention.

Grapes into gold – the alchemy of fermentation

At the start of fermentation, there may be some oxygen close to the juice, and in this situation, the yeast transforms sugar and oxygen into carbon dioxide and water (for chemists, the formula is $C_6H_{12}O_6 + 6O_2 = 6CO_2 + 6H_2O$). However, once all the oxygen has been used up, the yeast converts the sugar into alcohol and carbon dioxide ($C_6H_{12}O_6 \rightarrow 2C_2H_5OH + 2CO_2$). The carbon dioxide released then does an effective job of keeping oxygen away from the fermenting juice.

But what of the whole berries which currently take up most of the space in the vat? The carbon dioxide also has an effect on these. In the oxygen-free environment, a process known as carbonic maceration begins, in which a type of fermentation takes place within the grapes themselves. This generates alcohol, but also some flavour compounds which differ from those produced by normal fermentation. In many cellars in Beaujolais, they simply leave the grapes (Gamay, not Pinot Noir) in this vinous limbo in a closed tank for anything from a few days to a couple of weeks, and the result is the bright, fruity and slightly banana-y wines for which the region has become famous.

However, this is the Côte d'Or, not Beaujolais, and while a small amount of carbonic maceration can add an extra nuance to Pinot Noir, its influence shouldn't dominate the wine. So twice a day, most of the vats at Jadot are plunged. As well as the rotating pump, La Sablière is equipped with a rotating hydraulic plunger which can be positioned above each vat. At the flick of a switch, a device like a flat steel hand descends, squashes down the mass of grapes, and then rises. A quarter turn and it's on its way down again. The procedure is repeated four more times, and then the plunger is moved on to another vat.

Plunging has a number of effects. At this early stage in the fermentation, it crushes some more grapes, and mixes the solids in with the barely fermenting grape juice. Converting sugar to alcohol

NOT LIKE THAT, LIKE THAT
Whereas Bordeaux and Burgundy can point to centuries of experience, the history of quality wine in the Languedoc is much shorter, and the producers are still learning what does and doesn't work. 1998 was a great year in the region, but while several very good, even great red wines were made, many others were over-extracted at the maceration stage. Over-extraction occurs when the winemaker overworks the grapeskins in an effort to obtain more flavour, but in the process manages to extract bitter tannins and other unwanted polyphenols (think what happens if you stir those tea leaves too much). Lessons learned then have stood the winemakers in good stead. The grapes in 2000 were treated much more gently, and the wines are all the better for it.

is an important part of the period in the vat, but it's not the only thing going on. This is also the time when the flavours, colours, tannins and other compounds are extracted from the grape skins (and stalks if they are there) through maceration.

Packing the flavour in

Maceration is yet another well-debated topic. In some cellars, the grapes are crushed and then the mass of juice and skins is chilled and left for a cold soak (an alternative is to blanket the vat with sulphur dioxide, which inhibits yeast activity). Proponents say that the flavours obtained by doing this maceration before any alcohol has been made are finer than those released later on in the fermentation. No, no, say others, the best flavours are obtained during fermentation, providing the temperature in the vat doesn't rise above / fall below X °C. Still, others feel that post-fermentation maceration is the route to follow, since it is alcohol rather than water which is best at extracting all the good bits. It can be risky though, since without carbon dioxide being released, oxygen can get in and begin to turn the wine to vinegar. Again, great and not so great wines emerge from each camp, and it is experience more than anything else which dictates a winemaker's policy on maceration. In Jacques's case, experience has taught him that interfering as little as possible is the best approach.

With not too many crushed berries, the fermentation starts slowly. The gauges on the vats creep up little by little as more grapes split and release their juice, but even after the fruit has been in the vat for five days, there are still plenty of whole berries around (not to mention the odd very dead and very bloated caterpillar, but you didn't really want to know that). These berries

Below. Take the plunge. *The mechanical plunger is carefully positioned above each vat, and then allowed to do its work, breaking up the cap and mixing it in with the young wine beneath*

are not quite as dark in colour as when they were picked, as much of their pigment has been leached out into the vat. Taste one, and it's fizzy from the carbon dioxide.

During the first days of fermentation, plunging was fairly easy. The whole grapes were squashy, and as the paddle descended through them, they would either squish out of the way or get crushed. By now, however, there's more grape-juice-cum-virgin-wine at the bottom of the vat, and more of a mass of skins at the top, forming what is known as the cap. Since the cap is where all the flavour is, it's now more important than ever that it is regularly plunged to mix it with the liquid so that maceration can take place.

Plunging isn't the only way of making sure the cap stays wet. Pumping over is practised in many wineries: the juice from the bottom of the tank is pumped back into the top, often through

Right. A question of control. *The temperature of the stainless steel vat can be regulated via this keypad. Hot water or cooling brine can be circulated through the bands visible to the right of the console*

an attachment rather like a large shower-head. Another way of approaching this is to have either wooden boards (heading boards) or a stainless steel grille fixed in the tanks to keep the cap below the surface of the liquid.

Guillaume de Castellane has been experimenting with heading boards this vintage at Château des Jacques, and is pleased with the results, but as yet the method hasn't been tried at La Sablière. However, Jacques does have at his disposal yet another alternative to plunging. In the outer circle of vats are half a dozen horizontally mounted steel tanks called rotary fermenters or rotofermenters. These are sealed vessels which can be rotated, or which have internal paddles which themselves rotate, as often as the winemaker desires, thus mixing the cap in with the juice at regular intervals. The carbon dioxide is released through a one-way escape vent.

Rotofermenters are often used when the fruit needs to be processed as quickly as possible. Think of making a cup of tea. The more you stir up the tea (either loose leaves or in a bag), the quicker it brews. True, the end cuppa may not be as delicately flavoured as one which had brewed without stirring, but for those in a rush, it works. Similarly, if a winemaker wants maceration and fermentation to be over in a matter of days rather than weeks (he might need the vat space, for example), he can programme the rotofermenter to rotate every hour or so, and then leave it to get on with its business. Five days later, deep-coloured, fully fermented wine is pumped out, the tank is cleaned, some more grapes are put in and whole cycle begins again.

But that's only one way of using them. If the frequency of rotation is reduced, then the extraction is slower, and the fermentation takes place at a more gentle pace. This is the way Jacques uses his, giving them a turn twice a day, and keeping the wine in there for as long as in his regular vats. He's happy with the results, and has no qualms about putting some of the grands crus in the rotofermenters. 'After all, we have to put them somewhere.'

If there's one thing human feet are really useful for...

Most of the tanks, however, get their twice-daily plunge from the hydraulic device, which can be adapted to fit the differently sized tanks by adding or pulling off extra flaps. Even so, it's too large to fit into the six small wooden vats of the inner circle, so these have to be done manually, using something which looks like a large sink plunger. Sometimes, the cap gets so dry that even this won't do the job properly. In such instances there's nothing for it: a gullible student has to be persuaded to disrobe and leap into the vat to break up the grape skins by foot.

Ah, here comes a gullible student, Sebastian, fresh from the sorting table. He's been fortunate this year, and has only had to strip down to his wherewithals on two occasions. This method may be archaic, but it does have one advantage over mechanical systems. Within the vat, there will be pockets where the fermentation is especially vigorous. Sensitive feet can kick the ferment around and mix these hot-spots in with the rest of the juice.

THE RULES IS THERE IS NO RULES

A small amount of Ashley's wine is fermented off-site in lined concrete tanks, but at La Baume itself, everything is made in stainless steel. 'What interests us is good grapes, and we use a vast range of techniques aimed at getting the best flavours out of each batch. We can regulate the fermentation temperature in each tank according to the fruit. We allow Cabernet Sauvignon to begin fermentation straight away, but with Syrah, we'll chill down the must and gives the skins a few days of cold soak before fermentation starts.

Vinification vehicles

The shape of the vats also has an influence on the fermentation. Narrow, tall vats offer much less contact between the juice and the cap than wide, shallow ones, and so are not ideal for red wines. But wide, shallow vats also take up lots of floor space, so there has to be a compromise. At La Sablière, the height of the vats tends to be slightly greater than their diameter.

Temperature of fermentation is yet another variable to consider. Yeasts won't work below around 10°C, and are killed by temperatures greater than 45°C, but it's possible for fermentation to proceed at any point between these two extremes, even if the wines produced will differ greatly. Lower temperatures emphasise bright, fresh, fruit aromas and flavours, while higher temperatures can put the accent on cooked, sometimes stewed, characteristics.

Red wines are generally fermented at higher temperatures than whites, since these speed up the extraction of colour, tannin and flavour from the skins, but quite how high the upper limit is depends on the individual in charge of the fermentation. In this

Left. Jacques be nimble. *Backed by a bank of rotofermenters, Jacques wonders whether he has too many grapes to fill this tank*

Below. Sample test. *Each vat is tested regularly throughout the fermentation to check its progress and to ensure that the wine remains in good condition*

instance, it is Jacques Lardière, and – unsurprisingly – his opinions differ sharply from those of many people. Many winemakers treat Pinot Noir with kid gloves, and turn on the cooling systems if the temperature rises above 30°C. Not Jacques. 'I don't make fruity wines. I don't want to make fruity wines. Anyone can make fruity wines, but if I were to do so, I would not be respecting my customers. The fruit is only part of the plant. In order to push the wine to the maximum, you need to be outside the fruit, outside the immediate pleasure, and for that, you need heat. Heat is everything.'

In practice, this means leaving the fermentations alone, and not being too concerned if they occasionally hit a high 40°C. Not that this is a common occurrence. The ambient temperature in Burgundy during the vintage is not high – in fact, winemakers often have to heat their cellars in order to kick the fermentations off at all. The fermentation vats are seldom very large, so they have a relatively high surface-area-to-volume ratio, which helps to dissipate heat faster, especially if they're made from stainless

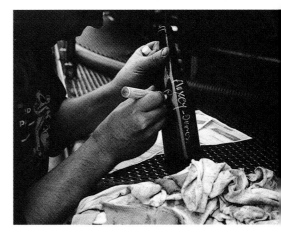

steel. This is one reason why some producers in the cool cellars of Burgundy prefer heat-retaining wooden vats.

The fermentation hall at La Sablière is actually above ground but, thanks to efficient extractor fans, it is never warm, even on the hottest days of the vintage. So the ferments bubble away, generating heat – and you can feel it if you put your head over one of the open vats (taking care not to be overcome by CO_2 and end your days in the vat), or stick your hand into the cap – but then losing it to the surrounding air. Jacques is content with this basic form of temperature control. 'It works, why meddle with it?'

Now, concentrate...

This doesn't mean that he's not open to alternative ideas. You have to keep experimenting, even if you often come back to the traditional ways. So for the 2000 vintage, Jadot is doing trials with a reverse-osmosis machine, a high-tech device used to concentrate wines. In this apparatus, wine and pure water are placed either side of a membrane which has pores large enough to allow water molecules through but too small for alcohol molecules. Pressure is applied to the wine side, and this forces the water molecules in the wine through the membrane, leaving a more concentrated liquid on the wine side.

The trial is being done on wine which has been macerating for about a week. By this stage, the fermentation is underway, and the wine/juice has a healthy ruby colour. However, since it is only a quarter of the way through its maceration, it only has a fraction of the flavour (and colour and tannin) it eventually will have. After

the reverse osmosis, the water is discarded, and the wine added back to the vat it came from. Rather than experiment with a simple bourgogne rouge, Jacques has chosen to use a small batch from the grand cru Clos Vougeot. 'And why not? We want to see the effect it has on the best.' Does he think he'll see an improvement in the wine? Another shrug. 'Maybe, maybe not. But it is important to be curious.'

Reverse osmosis is becoming especially popular in Bordeaux, where winemakers in some prestigious châteaux are using it to produce more concentrated wines, especially in those vintages when heavy rainfall around harvest time has diluted the grape juice. 2000 hasn't been a wet vintage in Burgundy, but the large crop, often of large grapes, means that some wines will lack a little intensity.

Those who don't have access to a reverse-osmosis machine can still do something to compensate for the deficiencies of nature (or those of their viticulture). A common Burgundian practice is to run off (or bleed off, as the French say) some of the juice from a vat early in the maceration process before it has had a chance to acquire much colour or flavour from the skins. This juice is then fermented to make a rosé wine called *saignée*, meaning 'bled', and what remains in the vat is more concentrated.

Sweet, but not quite sweet enough

The most common way of providing what nature couldn't is the process of enrichment or amelioration. This involves adding some form of fermentable sugar to the vat, either grape must of some sort or just simple sugar, in order to boost the final alcohol level. It is essential in the most extreme vine-growing climes of northern

LA BAUME

THE ACID TEST
Says Ashley: 'There's no such thing as a typical vintage here, and again I come back to the differences between 1998 and 1999. 1998 was a hot year, and there were many batches which we had to acidify in order to bring them into balance. 1999 was the opposite – we had to de-acidify the juice in several cases.' De-acidification is the addition of an alkaline substance, usually calcium carbonate, in order to neutralise the acidity. Chaptalisation is an alternative method of tempering high acidity, but it is prohibited in the Languedoc.

Below. Stick your nose in. *In the lab, Pierre-Henry and Christine make a nasal appraisal of how the new vintage is shaping up*

Europe. In England, for example, where grapes are often harvested with a potential alcohol level of less than 7%, producers are allowed to enrich their wine by 3.5% every year, and in really poor vintages by as much as 4.5%.

When sugar is used, as is the norm in Burgundy, the process is called chaptalisation, in honour of Jean-Antoine Chaptal, who was Napoleon's Minister of the Interior, and who popularised the process at the beginning of the 19th century. The Burgundians are allowed to chaptalise their wines by up to 2.5%, which many outside observers, not to mention plenty within the region, feel is excessive. To put this into context, if someone produces 4,000 cases of a wine a year, the equivalent of up to 100 of those cases can come from the sugar bag rather than the vineyard.

The subject of chaptalisation divides the Burgundians. Virtually all of them agree that using the full quota every year is wrong, as the wines will become unbalanced, with the extra alcohol producing a hot sensation in the mouth. Having said that, many feel that the process can be beneficial to the wines, even in years where the natural sugar levels in the grapes are high. Adding sugar towards the end of fermentation prolongs the activity in the vat, meaning better extraction, while in the finished wine, even a small increase in the alcohol level can bring greater richness and smoothness.

Those who disapprove of chaptalisation say that such arguments are merely an excuse to mask the fact that the grapes lack flavour. If the producers had reduced their yields, then they would have had richer flavours and more sugar in the grapes in the first place. Also, the use of chaptalisation arose at a time when less was known about how to deal with problems in the vineyard. When September came, the growers were anxious to pick their grapes as soon as possible before they lost significant amounts of them to pests and fungal diseases. With better viticulture, grapes can now be picked later with naturally higher sugar levels, so there's no need to resort to quite so much of Tate & Lyle's finest.

Hot sugar, cool acid

But while the grapes may be sweeter and riper, they are also lower in acidity. In addition, the widespread use of artificial fertilisers from the 1950s onwards has contributed to the general lowering in acidity levels. This has left many soils with high levels of potassium, which neutralises acid. So what? It's all to do with structure.

Compared with other grape varieties such as Cabernet Sauvignon and Syrah, Pinot Noir isn't especially high in natural tannin, so many wines rely on acidity to give them a backbone. If that acid isn't there, the wines can be dull, flabby even.

As a result, the need in some Burgundian cellars today is not just to chaptalise wines but to acidify them as well. This is permitted under law, providing producers don't do both processes to the same batch of wine. The logic of this is not apparent, since there's nothing to stop an acidified vat and a chaptalised vat being blended together at a later date. If acid (usually either tartaric or citric) is to be added, it's best to do so as early in the winemaking process as possible, since it will be less noticeable in the finished wine. Tipping it into the crusher-destemmer is often the favoured option, since this ensures its dispersal through the vat.

Tuning to perfection

Something else which is commonly tipped in at the crusher is sulphur dioxide (SO_2), in the form of potassium metabisulphite. You'll see why in the next chapter, since SO_2 has a more important role in white wines than in reds.

Adding sugar, adding acid, adding sulphur dioxide... And you thought wine was just made from grapes. The trend in Burgundy now is for a reduction in the addition of all three, although it's doubtful whether the use of any of them will ever be abandoned. The situation today is certainly preferable to the state of affairs 50 years ago, when many red burgundies were enhanced by the addition of beefy wine from warmer climes such as the Rhône, southern France and Algeria. Not that these wines were poor – they were often delicious, and remain so to this day. But they weren't true burgundy.

Any additions are kept to a minimum at Jadot. The healthiness of the fruit in 2000 has meant that the amount of SO_2 used has been tiny, and the acid levels haven't needed adjustment. The vats have been monitored each day to see what need there is, if any, for chaptalisation. Some *cuves* have been boosted by up to 0.5%, while others have been left alone. Mathilde spends much of her day scurrying and clanking between the fermentation hall and the lab carrying a milk-bottle carrier full of samples. Her father's policy of hands-off winemaking works only because he and Christine constantly monitor what is happening at every stage of

PUMPOVER BEETHOVEN
Ashley plans to do trials with open top tanks in the 2001 vintage, but at the moment, all the red wines at La Baume are fermented in upright tanks with closed tops. In order to keep the cap wet, the technique of pumping over is practised, in which juice is pumped out of the bottom of the tank and sprayed over the cap at regular intervals. How long the maceration lasts depends on the characteristics of the grapes. However, Ashley isn't a great fan of letting the wines spend a long time on skins, so it's a rare wine which spends more than 10 days in tank. The fermentations are regulated throughout, with the temperature towards the end of the process being allowed to rise to 27–30°C.

WHEN'S THE NEXT DRAIN?
Ashley isn't a great enthusiast of post-fermentation maceration, so as soon as the main activity has eased, he drains off the new wine and send the skins to the press. Some of his compatriots back in Australia choose to do the pressing even before this stage. They'll often drain the wine from the tank before all the sugar has been converted to alcohol, and then put it into barrel to complete the fermentation. They figure that colour and flavour in their wines are seldom a problem, so extended maceration doesn't add much to what is there already, and that by taking the wine off its skins at this early stage, they'll end up with something softer and more approachable.

fermentation in each vat. Their main concern in 2000 is the progress of the Marsannay from the hail-affected sites. The sorters have done what they can to cut out any bunches which showed signs of rot, and so far there's no evidence of off-flavours in the wines, but it's important to keep checking them.

If the hat fits, the vat'll wear it

As fermentation progresses, the cap dries out further, and plunging becomes increasingly difficult. After two weeks, most of the sugar has been converted to alcohol, but the fact that the cap is still being buoyed up by carbon dioxide shows that there's still some activity beneath the surface. Soon the cap will begin to break up and fall to the bottom of the tank. Many growers take this as a signal that it's time to drain the juice off and press the skins, but Jacques likes to leave the vats for as long as possible before pressing. Even the lowliest wines spend more than three weeks in vat, and some are left for up to five weeks. Since there is no CO_2 released during the final stages of maceration, each vat now wears its own made-to-measure, trampoline-like lid to protect it from oxygen.

These stretchy hats stay on until Jacques decides that each vat has had enough of a soak, and then it's time to remove the new wine. A pipe is attached to the outlet at the bottom of the vat, and the wine is gently drained into a holding tank. The skins left behind need pressing, since they still contain much in the way of colour, tannin and flavour. While many can be pumped into the press, someone usually has to get into the vat with a shovel to finish off the job.

Piling the pressure on

The traditional style basket press can still be found in many Burgundian wine cellars. This is rather like a straight-sided barrel with gaps between the staves and a flat disc inside that is forced downwards under pressure from man, animal or hydraulic power, with the juice running out through the gaps into a tray below. Modern presses work in a broadly similar fashion, but the barrel is usually made of perforated steel and is mounted horizontally. The pressure is exerted either by a moving head or by inflating a large internal airbag.

This second type is often known as a bladder press, and its action is particularly gentle. It's important to extract the goodness from

the skins, but it's equally important not to press too vigorously, since this could split the seeds and release bitter, more unpleasant-tasting tannins. The result of the pressing is called, not surprisingly, the press wine. Compared with the free-run wine, it's deeper coloured, more tannic and slightly less refined in flavour – not every winemaker will choose to use it.

The grapes are often given more than one pressing, since the first squeeze doesn't extract everything. However, the wines released get coarser and coarser each time, and Jacques prefers to blend these in with lesser wines. But he keeps the first pressing, since it's usually of a high quality. Will it all be blended in with the free-run? We'll see in Chapter 7.

Above. Hose were the days.
Perched on a ladder, the balletic Jacques positions the hose over the entry hole of Vat 81

white wine

'The flavour explosion of Sauvignon Blanc's crisp, flinty, tropical fruit is my strongest memory of my unforgettable days making white wine in New Zealand. Chile's whites are now just as distinctive, with Casablanca Valley providing a new interpretation of terroir for Sauvignon Blanc.'

*IGNACIO RECABARREN,
CHILEAN WINEMAKER*

Chefs treat white flour and brown flour in a broadly similar fashion, and white grapefruit and pink grapefruit in much the same way. So it would seem reasonable to expect there to be little difference between the processes for making decent wine from red grapes and those for making decent wine from white grapes. Wrong. White grapes can of course be treated in a similar fashion to red ones, and the outcome will be a wine of sorts. But just try drinking it...

It's all to do with skin. More specifically, it's all to do with substances called polyphenols in grape skins. Polyphenols exist in the fleshy bit of the grape (the pulp), but they're much more abundant in the skin. They include, amongst other things, tannin, flavour and colour compounds (remember phenolic ripeness in Chapter 3?). They're soluble in water and even more so in alcohol, so the longer the grape skins remain in contact with the juice after crushing, the more polyphenols are leached out.

The chemistry of polyphenols is still something of a mystery to the research scientists, and is way, way beyond the scope of this book (not to mention its author). But broadly speaking, in red grapes, some of the tannin and colour compounds react together to produce pigmented tannins, which are responsible for the colour of the eventual wine. In white grapes, there are far fewer colour compounds, so the tannins leave an unpleasant, harsh, bitter taste in the wines. This is why the juice of white grapes is separated from the skins early on in the winemaking process.

(It is perfectly possible to make white wine from red grapes. Anyone who has ever been bored enough to peel a red grape will know that - unless it is of the red-bodied Teinturier branch of the family - the flesh inside looks no different from that of a similarly naked white grape. If a winemakercrushes red grapes and presses them immediately, he'll get white juice, since there will have been no time for the colour to bleed out of the skins. This practice is often used in cooler climates where phenolic ripeness is difficult to achieve.)

Not that all contact between the grape juice and the skins is bad. A brief encounter – anything between 4 and 48 hours – can usefully add flavour and aroma to wines destined to be drunk within roughly two years of the vintage. Beyond this, the aromas fade and that bitterness comes to the fore.

Beauty starts in the vineyard

But Jacques makes wines for the long haul, so he has no truck with such methods. His efforts to eliminate any period of skin contact begin in the vineyard.

The modern plastic containers into which the Jadot pickers drop their bunches of grapes may not have the bucolic appeal of the traditional cone-shaped, back-borne wicker baskets which can still occasionally be seen around Burgundy's vineyards during harvest

Opposite. Turn of the screw.
White grapes are slowly pushed in the direction of the pump which will whisk them off into the press

LA BAUME

CHILL OUT
If temperature control at La Baume is important for red wines, then it's even more important for whites. It begins with the night picking, and continues once the grapes have arrived at the winery and been pressed. The juice is always chilled prior to fermentation, and once the yeast has been added, the chilling jackets built into each tank ensure that temperatures never rise too high. 'We try to adapt our ferments to the fruit we have,' says Ashley, 'but in general our ferments are very cool – 13°C is perhaps the max.'

LA BAUME

JUICY, JUICY

'We're juice makers,' says Ashley. 'I believe that good white wine starts with good juice, and that if you get your juice right before fermentation starts, then you won't have problems later on. When we receive grapes, we'll crush them and then analyse the juice. It may be that we have one batch which has lots of flavour but which lacks acidity, and another alongside which does have the acidity, then we'll blend them together before the fermentation starts. We do cold settling to separate the juice from the solids, but in some cases, if we feel it is right, we'll add some of the solids back. But again, it's a case of treating every batch on its own merits.'

time, but they are there for a reason. Several reasons in fact. For starters, they're easy to clean, and easy to stack in the back of a rented van. But more importantly, they're shallow, so once they're full, the fruit at the bottom of the containers isn't crushed under the weight of the grapes on top. In the mayhem of harvesting, when the interval between picking in the vineyard and processing at the winery could be several hours, this is crucial.

Saying no to machines

The need to have as little skin contact as possible means that mechanical harvesting is far from ideal for those seeking to make high-quality, long-lived white wines. Even the most gentle machines break some of the skins, and by the time the grapes arrive at the winery, the juice released will have begun to extract the polyphenols from the skins. Those who do pick white grapes by machine are now seeking to reduce this unwanted period of skin contact by having pressing equipment in the vineyards, but this is far from universal.

Anyway, Jacques is a firm believer in hand picking and in separating the juice from the skins as swiftly as possible. This explains why the sorters aren't being especially vigilant as the white grapes travel up the sorting table: the contact with the grape skins will be minimal. A few badly rotten bunches are weeded out, but those which are only partially affected by botrytis are allowed to continue along the conveyor belt. In wetter vintages, they would be more vigilant, but in a friendly vintage like 2000, the vast majority of grapes are ripe and healthy.

The yellow kid gloves...

From the conveyor belt, the grapes go into the crusher-destemmer and are then pumped straight into the press. Some of the smaller batches don't even make it onto the sorting table. They are transferred into the press, stalks and all, via a rather primitive small pump held together by those stretchy, stripy rubber 'spiders' more commonly seen on car roof-racks.

As the pressing starts, a smell akin to fresh apple peel begins to float around the winery. However, it's masked by the gagging pungency of sulphur dioxide (SO_2). White wines are more fragile than reds, and need to be protected from excessive oxidation, which can mute the aromas and turn the juice brown – think of what

happens to an apple after it's been peeled. Hence the addition of SO_2, which reacts with oxygen.

Saying no to sulphur

But while it's important to use sulphur, it's equally important not to use too much of it. First of all, it inhibits the action of the natural yeasts, which may be a plus point at some wineries, but not at La Sablière.

Secondly, it gives many people headaches and can leave some unpleasant characteristics in the wine. If sniffing a wine has ever caused you to wheeze, then sulphur dioxide is the component that is to blame. Worse, if the wine smells of rotten eggs, then the SO_2 has been converted into hydrogen sulphide (H_2S), and the winemaker hasn't been able to eliminate this characteristic before the bottling process.

A third reason for not being too heavy-handed with the SO_2 is that a small amount of oxidation can actually improve some wines. With aromatic grape varieties such as Riesling, winemakers do all they can to preserve the fragrances, and go to great lengths to exclude any contact with oxygen. But with more 'vinous' varieties, things are different.

Chardonnay, the grape that is used for all great white burgundies, is not especially aromatic, and exposing this grape to air at this early stage can bring out additional flavours in the finished wine. So Jacques flings some SO_2 in, but considerably less than is used in many cellars. 'Normally, if you keep the winery cool, and you keep it clean, then you don't need to resort to science as much.'

Below. Frothing at the mouth.
Not a rabid wine, but certainly one in which fermentation has set off at a cracking pace

Left. Tanked up. *Those who suffer from vertigo need not apply for jobs as winery workers*

Pressing matters

Pressing white grapes is more difficult than pressing red ones, since they are still full of sticky, unfermented sugar. As the bladder inside the press is inflated and the pressing begins, the first juice begins to emerge from the base of the machine and is pumped off into a tank. Well, it is if someone remembers to put the tray in the correct place underneath to catch the juice. (Those seeking to avoid any oxidation often have fully enclosed presses.) Skin contact at this stage is unavoidable, but it's only for the short time that the fruit is in the press.

The first juice to emerge is the best, and is fairly clear, but as the pressure is increased, the juice becomes more and more cloudy – until Jacques decides it's time to stop. At this stage, there's still some juice in the grapes, but the extra pressing needed to remove it would also extract some of those unwanted polyphenols. As with the reds, the final pressings are kept separate and used for lesser wines.

Cleaning up

Then comes the delightful job of cleaning out the press. Most of the mass of skin, stalks and seeds falls straight out of the

LA BAUME

REDUCTIONS IN STORE

'We're trying to make good fruity wines, so we do all we can to eliminate oxidation,' says Ashley. 'However, that doesn't mean that we pile in with the sulphur. In fact we do all we can to eliminate it altogether, and once again, the temperature control plays a big part in this. It's inevitable that there will be a bit of oxidation in the crusher, but before and after that, we look after the juice and the wine with kid gloves.

111

bottom into a waiting bin, but the last few remnants have to be scraped out and swept up with a good old-fashioned brush and shovel. This task often seems to fall to the cheerful Philippe. No wonder he drives that fork-lift truck like a maniac.

Splendid suspensions

The juice from the press is now transferred to a tank until fermentation starts. An option at this point is to chill the juice down to allow the suspended solids to drop to the bottom of the tank, and many winemakers add a selection of special enzymes at this stage in order to hasten this process. Alternatives to this 'cold settling' are filtering the wine, or putting it through a centrifuge, both of which processes remove solid matter efficiently.

But Jacques is firmly against all such procedures: he wants as many of those floaters as possible to be present for fermentation. 'They are part of the wine – it is crazy to remove them.'

Removal of the solids also invariably means that cultured yeasts have to be added to kick off the fermentation, and Jacques would much rather rely on the natural yeasts. They haven't let him down yet.

The power of oak

Once the juice is in the tank, fermentation starts fairly swiftly, especially if the grapes were warm to begin with. A small batch of Meursault which has been in one of the newly hired tanks for only a matter of hours has already developed a frothy head rather like a giant wobbly prawn cracker. Christine bustles up to deal with it. It's time for it to be transferred to barrel.

This is another stage that differs massively from the red wine fermentation. Fermenting red wine in a small barrel (the typical size in Burgundy is 228 litres) is not an option, since the mass of skins that would gather at the top of the barrel, plugging the bung-hole, would make monitoring the whole process a complete nightmare. A few winemakers sometimes drain the juice off the skins before fermentation has finished and then transfer the almost-finished wine into a barrel to complete the process, but performing the whole operation in small barrels is just not possible. However, there's no such problem with white wine, since all the skins have been removed, and all the whites at La Sablière are fermented in barrels.

Left. Now you robots, pay attention. *Jacques and Christine stand still for a rare moment to discuss the progress of the vintage*

Fermenting in barrel is in no way the easiest way to make wine. That single small tank of Meursault will soon be dispersed among five different barrels, while some of the larger cuvées will end up in 20, 50, even 100 different casks, each of which requires regular attention. Wouldn't it make more sense just to leave the juice to ferment in the tank?

Who said life was easy?

To economists and time-and-motion experts, yes. To wine-lovers, no, especially when it comes to less aromatic varieties such as Chardonnay which marry well with oak.

There's nothing to stop wines being fermented in large vessels made of either wood or stainless steel, and many producers, even in Burgundy, choose to follow this path. Modern stainless steel tanks even have in-built cooling systems to regulate the temperature inside.

In general, cooler temperatures (as low as 10°C) produce more aromatic but simpler wines, while higher ones (up to 22°C) make for something more complex but less fruity. Once the desired level has been set, the fermentation can be left to get on with itself, and winemaker can put his or her feet up.

The results can be good, sometimes very good. But for those who want to make great white wine in the Côte d'Or (not to mention in Carneros in California, in Australia's Yarra Valley, or New Zealand's Marlborough region, and in many other havens of fine Chardonnay besides), then, for these winemakers, only barrels will do.

Why barrels are better

The small size and therefore relatively large surface area of a barrel means that in a cool cellar, the temperature within the cask never rises to problematic levels. However, it is the ways in which barrel fermentation affects the character of a wine which make the major difference.

A Chardonnay which has been fermented in tank and then transferred to barrel for a period of ageing is much less subtle, and much more overtly woody, than one which has been aged and fermented in barrel. It is thought that the yeast reacts both with the flavour molecules in the wood to soften their impact, and also with the complex sugars which are on the inner surfaces of the barrel because of the toasting process. (Toasting? There's much more about barrels in Chapter 7.)

Another way in which barrels bring complexity is that where there was once just one tank of Meursault, there will soon be five mini-Meursaults, each of which will ferment in a slightly different fashion, to produce five similar but separate wines. When these are eventually blended back together, the result is usually greater than the sum of the parts.

A place to sleep

So barrels it is. There's not much evidence of these on the ground floor at La Sablière, but we did see a few in Chapter 4 disappearing down the lift into the underground cellars. Let's go downstairs and have a look for them. This huge basement has a splendid vaulted ceiling and even a small tasting room with built-in spittoons and a gravel floor. But it is the row upon row upon row of slumbering casks to which the eye is drawn. There's space down here for 5,000 barrels, and it's almost full. Many of the casks still hold wines from 1999, but for the present, everyone's attention is on the current vintage.

How many barrels?

One of the cellar hands is pumping the final drops from a batch of St-Aubin into the last of a long line of barrels, while two of his colleagues are checking with Christine which barrels to use for the soon-to-arrive Meursault. From the size of the tank, they know how many they're going to need, but they have to make sure they have the correct age and type of cask. Jadot renews only around 30

GIMME SOME SKIN
With most white grapes at La Baume, Ashley doesn't use skin contact. Is this because they've had some on the trip back to the winery after being machine-harvested? 'No way! Listen, when people talk about skin contact and mechanical harvesters, they're talking about ten years ago. Modern machines pick into small bins, and when you look in those bins, there's nothing sloshing about in the bottom. We get very grumpy if there is. Our fruit usually has sufficient flavour not to need it.'

Opposite and below. In the final analysis. *During the fermentations of both red and white wines, regular analysis means that problems can be dealt with as soon as they arise*

per cent of its white wine barrels each year, and there are barrels in the cellar which have been used once, twice, even three or four times before.

The decision on the balance between new and used oak depends on the quality of the fruit. Conventional opinion is that the better the wine and the vintage, the more able it is to support the flavours and tannins of new wood, so more new barrels can be used. But here, as in many things, Jacques is not conventional. His argument is that if the wine is very good, it doesn't need the extra flavour or structure which new wood brings, so he prefers used casks. Conversely, it is the poorer vintages and lesser wines which need a boost, so he increases, rather than decreases, the proportion of new barrels. And when you taste through the wines, you can't but agree that his philosophy works.

House-keeping

The best way to keep used barrels in good condition is to make sure they remain full of wine. Once they're empty, they're prey to bacterial infections which could affect any subsequent wine put into them. To minimise this risk, the casks are rinsed with water, and then disinfected by suspending a burning wick of sulphur inside each via the bung-hole. The barrels are then stored bung-hole down until it's time to use them, at which point they're rinsed out again. New casks come in a protective wrapper and should in

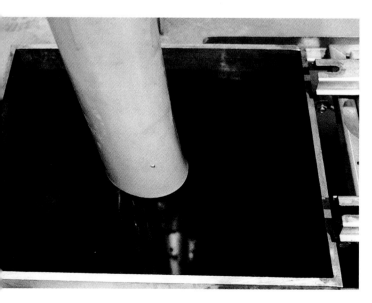
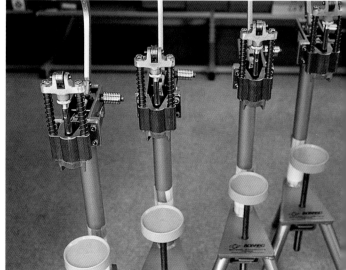

theory be ready to use straight away, after a quick rinse. Nevertheless, some producers prefer to fill them with hot water and give them a shake, so the steam can take the edge off some of the rougher wood flavours.

Getting the right recipe

For the Meursault, Christine has specified one new cask, two one-year-old casks, and two two-year-old casks, and these are now rolled into place ready for the wine, with their bung-hole uppermost. Then it's just a case of attaching one end of a hose to the tank, making sure the other end reaches the barrels, and turning on the pump.

Fermenting in barrel...

Since the cellar is below the level of the tank, the pump doesn't have to work too hard, and the five barrels are soon full. Well, almost full. Some space is left at the top of the barrel so that the yeast has some room (and some air) in which to begin working its magic and so that once fermentation really does gets going, the cask doesn't overflow.

For the first stages of fermentation, there's no need to put a bung in the top of the barrel, and even if you did, the pressure from the carbon dioxide would soon blow it out again. Underground cellars can be remarkably hazardous places at this time of year. During fermentation, a litre of juice generates around 50 litres of carbon dioxide; in the past, several winery workers have died in poorly ventilated cellars.

Chilling out

After a few days, when the fermentation has slowed down to near stopping point, bungs with airlocks are put into the barrels. The occasional 'blop' of CO_2 escaping through the airlocks shows that there's still some activity in the barrel, and this can continue for weeks, even months. This isn't good news for those seeking to sell their wine as soon as possible, although such producers would be unlikely to find themselves chewing their nails in this situation as they'd usually rely on an efficient cultured yeast to finish off the fermentation as quickly as possible. But for those who prefer to let nature run its course, then it's a question of sitting and waiting.

Above. Just a spoonful of sugar...

A tank of white wine receives its chaptalisation

In particularly cool cellars, wines can still be fermenting in the June after the vintage; in extreme cases, they'll still be bubbling away when the next vintage comes around. Not every bubble of CO_2 is a by-product of the conversion of sugar into alcohol. Wines go through a secondary fermentation, called the malolactic fermentation – more about that in the next chapter.

And much, much later...

It's the evening of 28 September, the day on which the final batch of grapes arrives at La Sablière...

Jacques's voice has descended maybe an octave during the course of the vintage, and his black Levi's are so full of sugar that they might start fermenting themselves. Christine's phone is threatening to fall apart, but she herself is in one piece, even if the mad glint of the dog-tired still appears in her eyes.

She's wearing a Robert Mondavi T-shirt, not out of choice, but because her original top got badly Pinot-ed during a tussle with a vat of recalcitrant Gevrey-Chambertin earlier in the day. 'Ah yes, they make very good wine, Mondavi.' As good as burgundy? A pause. 'They make good wine.'

The pair of them look like they need a week in bed (not together though), and even the normally immaculate Pierre-Henry appears to have passed several days without seeing either an iron or a comb. But all the grapes are in, there was enough tank space to take this year's large crop, and there has been no problem with flavours of rot in the Marsannay.

What will the future be?

Will the 2000 harvest turn out to be a great vintage? 'It is far too early to say', says Jacques. 'You think you can tell how good or how bad the wines are going to be, and then they surprise you. I know we will produce some very good wines, both white and red, but if you ask me at this stage which will be the best, I cannot tell you with certainty.'

It's only the first stage of the winemaking process that is over. The wines won't be bottled for many months, and before then, there's plenty of work for this trio to do. But at least tonight, for the first time in several days, there's a chance of all of them getting to bed before midnight.

style choices

'One of my favourite sayings is "making wine is a skill, fine wine an art." Once a winemaker has the skills, the choosing of styles creates winemaking art. And once you choose a style, a commitment to excel is a crucial factor. This is what I've tried to do all my life.'

ROBERT MONDAVI,
CALIFORNIAN WINEMAKER

According to the late, great, Peter Sichel of Bordeaux, the character of a wine is determined by its terroir, its personality by the vintage, but its quality is due to the influence of man. It's very fashionable for winemakers to say that they 'just let the wine make itself', or that they adopt a 'hands–off approach'. If this were so, then all their cellars would look the same, and all their Gevrey-Chambertins or Stellenbosch Pinotages or Wachau Rieslings would taste the same. And there'd be absolutely no need for this chapter.

LA BAUME

TO BLEND OR NOT TO BLEND
Jacques Lardière believes
that any blending should be done
as soon as possible, but Ashley
Huntington is more flexible. 'We
do our blending of juices prior to
fermentation for the white wines,
whereas for reds, we just treat
each parcel separately. But in
both instances, we still end up
with several tanks of wines which
at some point have to be blended
together. Precisely when we do it
is decided at the tasting bench.
Sometimes it will be just after
fermentation, but at other times,
it may only be a couple of months
prior to bottling.'

While there may be large differences between wines of similar origin, it is impossible to say that one style of wine is 'the best'. Jacques Lardière's way with both red and white wines is at odds with those of many of his Burgundian compatriots, but that's not to say that they are wrong and he is right, or vice versa. All good winemakers have their own strongly held beliefs, yet all are also prepared to concede that their neighbours and rivals makes wines which can be every bit as good. But different.

Style choices begin well before the end of fermentation. Much of the book so far has been about how decisions at various stages of the grape-growing and winemaking cycles ultimately affect the wine. Another favourite saying of the hands-off brigade is that 'great wine is made in the vineyard'. But this is a case of false humility on the part of the winemaker. While it's undeniable that the quality of the raw materials – grapes – sets the potential of a wine, it's down to the bloke who fiddles about with them to determine its actual quality. The coda to 'great wine is made in the vineyard' is 'ah yes, but great grapes can still get cocked-up in the winery'.

Rearing the wines

So far, Jacques hasn't *coqued*, sorry, cocked anything up. The red wines have finished fermentation and been pressed, while the whites are sitting snugly in their barrels in the cellar. The period between now and when the wines are finally bottled is called *élevage*, the same word that is used for the breeding and rearing of animals. Jacques's task over the next few months is to 'rear' his wines in the best way he knows.

This means making sure that they have a good home, and where top class burgundy is concerned, that means a decent barrel. Jadot buys over 1,000 new barrels each year, and at more than £300 each, that's a sizeable investment. If Jacques were to shop around, he could find barrels at half the price. So what's so special about the ones he chooses to buy? Indeed, what's so special about barrels in the first place? Why doesn't Jacques just bung the wine straight into a bottle and have done with it?

He could of course do this, but then he'd be betraying his responsibility to the terroir and to the vineyards to produce the best wine he possibly can. Think of a barrel as a good finishing school. The wine goes in an awkward adolescent, and comes out

'Another favourite saying of the hands-off brigade is that "great wine is made in the vineyard". But this is a case of false humility on the part of the winemaker'

Above. Tanks, and goodbye. *With the fermentation now over, both the wooden and stainless steel vats once again stand empty*

older and wiser. Its character and personality are still intact, but it is now a much more rounded, complete entity.

The perfect schooling

Before examining what an oak barrel actually does to a wine, let's take a look at how one is made. A measure of how seriously Jadot takes the whole subject of barrels is that the company has a 35 per cent stake in a local cooperage, Tonnellerie Cadus, established in 1996. A morning at Cadus, or indeed any cooperage, is a reassuring experience for those who struggle to keep up in today's high-tech world. While some of the work can now be done by computer-controlled equipment, at heart it's still the dirty, labour-intensive, time-consuming operation it has always been.

In charge of Cadus is Paquito Barbier, another stylish Frenchman whose standards of grooming are not too far behind those of his brother-in-law Pierre-Henry Gagey. 'This is our wood supply', he says, pointing to the pillars of staves which have been carefully arranged outside the factory not far from the hill of Corton.

The staves, arranged ten to a level and stacked 40 high, have each been checked by hand on arrival.

This may seem like a bit of a palaver for what looks like just a long thin plank. However, a barrel stave is a very special long thin plank. First of all, it's made of oak. Other types of wood can be used for barrels but no other has the combination of durability, pliability, impermeability and wine-enhancing flavours found in oak. Secondly, it's made from a special type of oak. There are several species of oak, and not all are suitable for wine. Red oaks, for example, are porous, so they're out. White oaks are better, and, broadly speaking, these can be divided into two types: American and European.

French vs American

American white oak is less porous than its European counterpart, so a log can simply be sawn into as many staves as its size permits. In contrast, the European oak needs to be cut or split so that the staves follow the line of the wood grain, otherwise the barrel will leak. As a result, around 75 per cent of a European oak tree is unsuitable for staves, and less than half as many staves can be obtained as from its American twin. This means that American oak

IT'S A FINE, FINE LIFE
Ashley's thoughts on fining and filtration are very much influenced by commercial considerations. 'In our game, you've got to produce a stable product which isn't going to go funny on a supermarket shelf. All our wines are filtered and stabilised to make them commercially presentable, but how each wine is treated differs depending on its character. Barrel ageing and racking mean that many wines emerge with reasonable clarity, but even so, everything is filtered. Having said that, I have far less against the people who say wine should not be filtered, than those who will only use wild yeast.'

Raw ingredients. *To make a barrel, simply take six hoops (far left), then add just the right number of staves (left) and just the right amount of heat (above)*

**Above. Assembling a barrel
in six easy lessons:**

1 *Staves are positioned round the
inside of the first hoop*

2 *A larger hoop is put over the first
and knocked into position, then the
initial hoop is hammered into place;
a third, smaller hoop is added for
the top*

3 *Adjustments are made along the
way to make sure the staves are
perfectly level*

4 *Now comes the hot bit...*

5 *The barrel to the right has been left
over a brazier for the wood to soften.
Meanwhile, a cooper checks that the
diameter of another barrel.is OK, and
then it's on to the next one*

6 *A barrel receiving its final toasting
– a lid keeps the heat in*

barrels are significantly cheaper than those made of European –
especially French – oak.

So why not use American oak barrels? A Frenchman's answer
would be: 'Because they are inferior'. And, historically, this has
certainly been true. A wine matured in American oak would have
had a sweeter, cruder flavour, with intrusive hints of vanilla and
coconut, compared with a wine matured in European oak. However,
it's now becoming clear that this has been more to do with the way
the barrels have been made than with the quality of the initial oak.

Also there is American oak and there is American oak, ditto for
European oak. From a winemaking point of view, the best of each is
marked out by the tightness of its grain, which is largely determined
by how quickly the trees grow, and how densely they are planted.
This, then, is the third factor explaining why a stave is not just a
long thin plank. The closely planted, slow-growing trees found in
the forests of central France have shown themselves to be ideal for
wine barrels – ideal, that is, apart from the fact they need to be
around a hundred years old before they're considered suitable for
barrel staves. There's no reason why their success will not be
duplicated one day in other parts of the world. At present, the oak
from French forests such as Allier, Nevers and Vosges is considered
to be the finest, although many wineries ordering barrels now tend
to specify not only the source of the oak, but also the tightness
of its grain per forest.

Drying and toasting

Factor number four is the way in which the oak has been seasoned. Once the staves have been cut, they need to be dried out. The traditional way is to stack them up outdoors and allow the process to take place naturally, but it can be dramatically speeded up by kiln-drying.

There is, however, a trade-off. If you look at a stack of staves which have been allowed to dry out in the open air, you'll see the ground below stained brown with the various substances, among them harsh flavour compounds and tannins, which have been leached out over the months of ageing. Air-dried oak has a much more subtle impact on wine than kiln-dried, and if American oak has been considered the poor cousin, it's because most of the wood has been kiln-dried. Left to themselves outdoors, the staves will take anything between one and three years to dry out naturally. What's more, long, gentle ageing in a temperate climate is preferable to a shorter, more intense spell in torrid conditions.

Add to all this the fact that the staves have been shaped for barrel making so that each end is narrower than the middle, and it soon becomes evident why by the time the staves arrive at Cadus after three years outside in the Cognac region, they cost around £7 each. Paquito is hoping that sometime soon, he'll be able to age his own wood on site, and thus cut his costs slightly, but high-quality oak will never be cheap.

Above. The finishing touches:

1 *Preparing the end of the barrel for its head*

2 *Yes, that is an old bath full of reeds*

3 *...they're used to make the barrel heads watertight but ever so slightly flexible*

4 *You've got have somewhere to put the wine in*

5 *The finished product...*

6 *...and several of its friends in their protective shrink-wrap*

Rolling out the barrels

Then there's the minor matter of turning those staves into a barrel. Barrel making starts at 6am each morning with the firing up of the burners over which the barrels will be shaped and toasted. Several sets of the six metal hoops which form a framework for the staves will have been made by someone else the previous day. The first job is to find a selection of staves which have the correct combined width to form the circumference of the barrel. These are then fitted, by hand of course, into one of the smallest hoops, so that the staves splay out like a hula-hula skirt. A second and larger hoop is then placed over the stave skirt and, with the aid of a hammer, is banged as far down the staves as it will go. A third hoop, larger still, follows.

With the staves now locked into position, it's time for the shaping to begin. Oak needs some form of heat to become pliable, and this can come from a variety of sources such as gas, steam, or, as at Cadus, a wood-chip burner. The barrel with its three hoops is placed over a burner and left to absorb the heat. It's important during this stage that the staves don't dry out too much, otherwise they might split, so a squirt of water is applied from time to time.

After about half an hour, the staves are ready for bending. The three hoops already in place will have been hammered slightly further down the barrel during the heating, causing some curvature in its top half, but it's now time to bring together the splaying ends of the staves. For this, a cable is wrapped round them and tightened. Slowly the staves bend to meet each other, and the cooper is able to

fit an initial hoop, and then two more, over the bottom end of the barrel, bringing the base into the same shape as the top.

A certain amount of charring inevitably occurs on the insides of the barrel during this process. Customers can specify whether they want any higher degree of 'toasting'. If they do, the barrel is now angled over the burner until its insides are high toast, medium toast, medium toast plus, or whatever is required.

And when it all goes wrong?

Uh oh. A stave in one of the barrels has split in the heating process. It happens – it's made of wood. Unfortunately, a cooper can't resort to glue on such occasions, so the hoops are bashed off, and the search is then on for a similarly sized stave left over from a previous faulty barrel to plug the gap. If the fit is good, there won't be much need to rebend the barrel. If not, it will need a little more time over the burners. Paquito may be based in Burgundy, but where barrels are concerned, he much prefers the 225-litre Bordeaux barrique to the 228-litre Burgundian *pièce*, simply because the latter is longer and narrower, so the staves are more likely to break.

Finishing touches

Once the barrel is bent and toasted to the cooper's satisfaction, it's rolled on for the next stage: the bung-hole is drilled through the centre of one of widest staves. You don't have to be an expert to spot a slight deficiency in the barrel at this point – it has no ends. Part of the solution lies in an old tin bath in an adjacent room. The bath is full of reeds which have been soaking there for a couple of hours. The barrel heads are made of staves pinned together with acacia wood, but the reeds are put between the staves to make sure that no wine seeps out of either end of the barrel. It works, don't knock it.

Because each barrel is hand made, the heads have to be individually shaped to fit. A groove is made on the inside of the barrel, and the heads are then planed to the required diameter. Fitting them involves loosening the hoops, applying a primitive paste made from flour, ash and water, and then coaxing the head into place. Once both ends have been done, the hoops are bashed down once more and the barrel is finished.

Or at least it looks finished to the untrained eye. It isn't. First of all it needs to be checked for leaks, so it's filled with boiling water

and shaken about for a time. Smaller holes can sometimes be plugged with an oak peg, which means removing only one of the heads, but larger ones mean the replacement of entire staves, which entails taking the barrel apart and starting again almost from scratch. Once there are no leaks, the barrel is finished.

Well, not quite. Its surface is still a little rough, so off come the hoops again, and the staves are sanded to a smooth finish. This time when the hoops go back on, they're riveted in place. Ask Paquito nicely, and you can have chestnut hoops rather than metal ones for only £24 extra. What's the difference? 'It used to be because they were easier to roll around the cellar, but now it's largely cosmetic. When people have a showcase winery, the chestnut doesn't scratch the expensive floors as much.'

The wood trade

Paquito aims to make barrels at a steady rate throughout the year, simply because it's impossible to speed up any of the processes involved at Cadus. 'The Americans all want theirs shipping in June and July when they have space in their wineries, so we have to try

Opposite and below. Class in the glass. *Colour, good. Nose, good. Taste, good. No machine can judge a wine as effectively as a skilled taster*

Right. Behind the flask. *Four suspect wines wait for analysis on Jacques's very expensive but fabulous machine...*

LA BAUME

BARREL OF FUN

'The whole subject of barrels is a fascinating part of winemaking,' says Ashley. 'What we're trying to do is build the wood to lift the wines, not smother them, and we've found that French oak works best for this. In the beginning, we did try some American oak, but we found that the flavour it gave the wines was just too much. This is France, not Australia, and even in the Languedoc, the wines tend to be a little drier with less forward fruit character. My favourite tastings of the year are the barrel tastings when you line up maybe 200 different wines which started life the same and then went into different barrels. The range of flavours is absolutely astonishing.'

and stockpile barrels, and estimate what the demand will be. But some producers seem to think that they can order a barrel one day and receive it in the post the next. They don't realise that we send everything by sea, unless they want to pay extra. Most shipments are taken initially by road to Rotterdam. It's the best way – the trains shake them to matches, and the French harbours are usually on strike.'

Even so, vintage time sees Cadus working flat out from 6am to 8pm. 'Everyone wants their barrels now, now, now. It's terrible.' The reward for his efforts is that when anyone enters a cellar full of his barrels, or those of another cooper, for a visit, they find it impossible to leave without touching, feeling, caressing even just one or two of them.

What you get on the nose and palate...

But barrels aren't there just to make cellars look pretty, so let's take a look at what happens when a wine is put into a barrel. First of all, the wood brings flavours to the wine. If you sniff a wine and detect aromas of coconut, vanilla, spice (especially cloves), or caramel, then the chances are that they are derived from substances which leach out of the oak. Their intensity varies according to the way in which the barrel has been made – in general, the cruder the coopering, the cruder the flavours will be in the wine. Higher levels of toasting can increase the intensity of some of these characteristics. The age of the barrel also has a significant impact, with the amount of flavour decreasing as the barrel gets older. Then there's its size. The smaller the barrel, the greater the ratio of surface area to volume, and the greater the intensity of the oak flavour.

It must be said that a woody overtone in a wine can be extremely attractive, providing it doesn't overwhelm the other flavours. There are now ways in which winemakers can add oaky flavour to wines destined to be drunk young without recourse to expensive barrels. One of these is to bung a large tea-bag-like affair stuffed with oak chips into a tank of wine, while another is to suspend a curtain of staves in the tank. Early wines made by both methods were coarse, but as the manufacturing techniques for each have improved, and winemakers have become more adept at using them, the wines have improved remarkably. The first chipped wines in particular used to stand out like a sore thumb in tastings, but today's examples are a distinct improvement, and can often be spotted only because of their low price tag.

(Don't say as much to a Frenchman. A well-known Bordeaux château owner said of the use of oak chips: 'Not only can it not replace barrel ageing, but it is a step towards savage and artificial aromatisation and flavouring. If you use oak chips to give flavour, what about blackcurrant syrup, colour elements or other ingredients?')

LA BAUME

CHIPS WITH EVERYTHING
Currently, the use of oak chips and barrel staves is illegal in France. Well, almost. 'It's daft,' says Ashley. 'You can apply to the government to do an official trial of up to 50,000hl of wine – that's almost twice as much our total production, so it's hardly a limited experiment.' So is he participating in these trials? 'You're kidding. And have loads of bureaucrats poking their noses into everything? In Australia, people use chips unashamedly, but here, you can get put in jail. I think that'll change though. I also think that when it does, you'll see some "interesting" wines. You only have to remember some of the dreadful stuff Australia made when chips were first used to realise that.'

Left. The blend is nigh. *When it comes to tasting the trial blends of red wine, the results are often greater than the sum of the individual parts*

Creating a good atmosphere

A barrel's role, however, extends beyond that of adding flavour. Already in Chapter 6 we've seen how the yeast was reacting with flavours and sugars on the inside of the barrel. This can of course be replicated by the use of oak chips and staves in a stainless steel vat, providing they are used early enough along the winemaking route. What cannot be replicated are the reactions that take place due to the gradual oxygenation of the wine. A barrel isn't intended to leak, but even so its staves are ever so slightly porous, and the wine 'breathes' through its sides. Air also gets in every time the bung is removed.

This gentle aeration causes many things to happen in the wine, especially to our friends the polyphenols. It rounds out aromas and flavours, and reduces the risk of development of unwanted stinky sulphur compounds such as hydrogen sulphide. It helps clarification

and, in red wines, it encourages the development of the pigmented tannins which provide the wines with colour and structure. These tannins gradually join together (polymerise is the technical term) to form longer and heavier chains, which eventually drop to the bottom of the wine to form sediment. That's why wines such as Rioja Gran Reserva which have spent a long time in barrel tend to be quite pale in colour.

At the moment, the wine going into barrel at La Sablière is a deep, vigorous, youthful purple. It's the 2000 Beaune Boucherottes, fresh from the tank on the storey above. Jacques thought the press wine was so good that he's blended it all in with the free-run. 'Normally, we try to blend as early as possible, as the wines need time to come together. If you keep the batches separate until just before bottling, the results are not as good.' As with the whites, around 30% of the barrels are new each vintage.

ST MALO

Just as Ashley doesn't trust natural yeasts for the alcoholic fermentation, so he'd much prefer to inoculate his wines for the malolactic fermentation. But not all of them. 'We never do any malo on Sauvignon Blanc, since it needs the extra acidity. For Chardonnay, we look at what we have and then decide. 1998 was a low acid year, so we only did a bit, while 1999 was much cooler, so we needed to do more. And of course we make sure the malo goes through for all the reds. We'll begin by inoculating one tank, and then once that's started, we'll transfer the lees from there other tanks to get them going.'

'Le malo'

The Beaune has finished its alcoholic fermentation, but it's now about to go through another fermentation called the malolactic, often abbreviated to 'malo' or MLF. Yeast doesn't play a part in the malo, which almost always takes place after the alcoholic fermentation. Instead, bacteria transform malic acid (think green apples) to lactic acid (think milk), with the overall effect of reducing the total acidity. As with the alcoholic fermentation, a producer can add substances to promote the malo, or rely on nature to take its course. It's no surprise that Jacques falls into the latter camp. A certain amount of heat is needed for the malo to take place, and in the cool cellars of Burgundy, it often comes to a temporary standstill over winter, only to begin again with the first flush of spring warmth. In the days before the process was fully understood, this was attributed to the rising of the sap.

Virtually all reds are put through the malo, the only exceptions being a few light wines intended for early consumption. In Burgundy, the malo usually takes place once the wine is in barrel, and this practice is becoming increasingly popular round the world. Performing the malo in barrel (as opposed to in an inert tank) makes for better integration between the wood and the wine, at least in the important early stages of a wine's life when the influential critics make their pronouncements. Ten years down the line, you may not be able to tell whether or not the malo took place in barrel, but by then, the wine will all have been sold.

The malo isn't as critical for white wines, and many producers choose to block it in all or part of their wine in order to preserve the acidity level. This is done by adding sulphur dioxide or by sterile filtration. If the malo isn't completed, it's important that all bacteria are removed before the wine is bottled, otherwise a refermentation could occur. When a total malo takes place in wines with very low acid levels, Chardonnays in particular, the results can be rather flabby, with unattractive buttery flavours very much in evidence.

All the reds at La Sablière complete the malo, but for whites, there's no absolute policy. Jacques tends to let every barrel progress at its own speed, and while many will complete the malo, others even from the same batch of grapes won't even begin theirs.

A consequence of the whites being fermented in barrel is that once fermentation has finished, there will be a sludgy layer of dead yeast cells and other detritus – known as the lees – at the bottom of

'A wine subject to pre-fermentation oxidation goes into barrel a mucky brown, but after a few months of bâtonnage, *the colour is much paler and clearer...'*

the cask. These lees need careful attention since if they are allowed to lie undisturbed, hydrogen sulphide can develop. The solution is to agitate them regularly by pushing a big stick through the bung-hole and giving the wine a good stir...

Stirring up trouble

This *bâtonnage*, as the French call it, has beneficial effects on the wine: it circulates the yeast and the lactic bacteria, which speeds up both the alcoholic and the malolactic fermentations. The lees act as a barrier between the wine and the wood, so the take-up of the coarser flavours from the wood is diminished. They also react with polyphenols in the wine, causing unwanted tannin and colour molecules to precipitate out. A wine which has been subject to pre-fermentation oxidation goes into barrel a mucky brown, but after a few months of *bâtonnage*, the colour is much paler and clearer. Because reds are fermented in vat, there isn't the same amount of lees in each barrel. Even so, *bâtonnage* is still useful both for stopping the development of H_2S and for encouraging completion of the malo.

Wines at La Sablière spend anything between 10 and 20 months in cask, depending on the characteristics of each wine, and during this time, most reds and whites will be racked just once. Racking is simply transferring a wine from one barrel to another, and it's done to aerate the wine, and also to remove it from the lees.

Racking all over the world

It's a sunny summer day, but downstairs in the cellar at La Sablière, a jumper is needed. Christine spots a couple of figures skulking in the shadows behind a four-high stack of barrels. 'I have two workers who have no work – I don't like that. Hey, come here!' After a terse discussion, the two are hastily dispatched for barrel-washing duty. Today is the day for racking the 1999 Beaune Boucherottes, which has been sitting in the same 30 barrels since the previous October.

There's some checking to do first, however. Christine suspects that the wine in some of the casks is not as good as it should be. The easiest way to determine this is to taste each one. Armed with a glass and a 'thief', the pipette-like instrument used for drawing wine from barrels, she sets off sniffing and spitting down the row. Sure enough, two of the barrels have the vinegary whiff of volatile acidity. On these, she chalks the initials AT for *à traiter*. In other words, the barrel needs treatment before it can be used again.

Samples of the two suspect wines are taken up to the lab for analysis on a super-duper machine which has simplified Jacques and Christine's workload remarkably. 'I love it', cries Jacques. 'It is very expensive but fabulous – just like burgundy!' In no time at all, the machine has confirmed that the volatile acidity is far too high, so Christine goes back downstairs and adds the initials NPP – *ne pas pomper*, or don't pump this one – next to the AT. Faulty wines such as this are sometimes blended away into lesser cuvées, although in this instance, they may just have to be poured away. The casks too may be beyond redemption.

It's time to begin racking the remaining 28 casks. A large funnel is placed in the bung-hole of an empty barrel, which is then positioned beneath a full one. The small hole in the head of the upper barrel is unstoppered, and the wine gushes out, hopefully into the funnel. A tap is hastily inserted into this hole, and the racking then proceeds at a more leisurely pace. When the upper cask is nearly empty, the funnel is taken away and replaced by a dish into which the last of the wine and the lees can be tipped. The procedure is then repeated for each of the remaining casks, and these are then manoeuvred into their designated place in the cellar

LA BAUME

FORM MONITOR

'With wines, we're working with living creatures, and things could go wrong at any time. I'd rather be a control freak and monitor a wine on every possible occasion than have it go funny on me. During fermentation, we're checking things twice a day, and once it's finished and in tank or barrel, we're still there twice a week. With our premium reds, we're racking them maybe four or five times during their time in barrel, which is 12–15 months depending on the vintage. But we never rack as hard as we can. The French government take 2% of all the wine we produce as tax, so we might as well give them that bit which we recover from the lees.'

after being taken away for rinsing. The lees are put in a centrifuge to extract the wine, and the residue from this is sent away to be distilled into Fine de Bourgogne, a type of brandy.

A quick look down the bung-holes along the new row of casks reveals that the barrels aren't full up – no surprise, since they've shed a few litres of lees in the racking process. The barrels need to be topped up, ideally with the same wine (although this isn't always possible). Topping up isn't done just at the time of racking. Natural evaporation means that the barrels lose a significant amount of their contents each year, even in a humid cellar, and it's important that the air which seeps in is kept to a minimum. A little is acceptable, a large amount could turn the wine to vinegar, so in order to prevent this, the barrels at La Sablière are topped up every ten days.

Barrel to bottle, at last!

Throughout the time the wines are in barrel, Jacques and Christine are constantly tasting the various casks, checking for any faults that might develop, checking to see how the wines are progressing, seeing if they can determine when each will be ready for bottling. Once they've decided a wine is ready, the contents of the barrels will be transferred to tank and allowed to settle there for a few days. The two will then examine the wine, which has clarified naturally during its stay in the barrel, and decide what treatment if any is needed.

Right. Lotta bottle. *Don't let anyone tell you that bottling lines are dull affairs. True, they all have much in common, but when they're in full flow, they're so mesmerising that you can sit and watch them for hours. Especially with a glass of something decent for company*

The subjects of fining and filtration of wine arouse great passion among wine-lovers. (Both processes are aimed at clarifying and stabilising the wine. With fining, a fining agent is used to speed up the precipitation of ultramicroscopic particles suspended in the wine. Filtration, on the other hand, strains out solid particles.) The outspoken Rhône vigneron Michel Chapoutier has said, 'Filtering wine is like making love using a condom'. Certainly, cack-handed fining and especially filtration can strip the soul from a wine, and even lightly filtered wines can suffer a loss of personality in the few months after bottling. However, if the wines aren't treated, there's the risk of bacterial spoilage, and even refermentation. Jacques doesn't fine his reds, but sometimes gives them a light filtration, while the whites are unfiltered, but receive a light fining with casein.

Then it's time for bottling. Jadot has a state-of-the-art, fully automated, sterile bottling line. In full flow, it's a mesmerising sight, washing, sterilising, filling and finally corking the bottles at the rate of more than one a second. Each cork bears the Jadot name, along with the vintage and the appellation of the wine it's intended for. And yes, they are made of real cork, not a synthetic substitute. Jacques and Pierre-Henry acknowledge that the failure rate of natural cork – anywhere between 2 and 10 per cent – is far from ideal, but they confess that they're both ardent traditionalists on this subject, as are most of their customers. So cork it is. Let's move on.

LA BAUME

WITH A TARGET IN MIND
Because of the commercial nature of his work, does Ashley feel under pressure to make his wines presentable earlier than he would like? 'Not at all. We have three ranges of wine – varietal, Sélection and Domaine la Baume – and when we receive a batch of fruit, we look at it with these in mind and treat it accordingly. We're constantly blending towards a target, and this helps us keep our minds focused. That is after all what we're paid to do.'

ageing & selling

'In order to produce great wine, you have to take risks, and sometimes they work, sometimes they don't. It would be very easy to make wines that were simple and correct, but because I respect the customer, I won't do that. When you aim for the highest level, the reality is that people will not like certain wines.'

JACQUES LARDIÈRE, LOUIS JADOT

There's an old joke which goes, 'How do you make a small fortune in the wine business? Start with a large one.' Many people forget that, with the exception of a few rich hobbyists, every wine producer needs to turn in a profit if it is to survive. It's no use making the finest Pinot Noir or Chardonnay or Cabernet Sauvignon in the world if, at the end of day, no one buys it. The wine trade is full of some awfully nice people making or selling awfully nice wines. Their knowledge of how to sell the stuff however could be balanced on the tip of a corkscrew.

Above. Put it in the bin. *If you're not in the know, you need to be a cryptologist to be able to work out the contents of the unlabelled bottles in this wooden bin*

'...there is an upper echelon of wines which, either through reputation or critical acclaim, will be snapped up almost regardless of their price. Others, however, need to be actively pushed'.

Not everything needs to be sold. In the wine hierarchy, there is an upper echelon of wines which, either through reputation or critical acclaim, will be snapped up almost regardless of their price. But below that lofty level, the competition is much fiercer. Wines from traditional European regions now have parvenus from the New World and southern Europe elbowing them off the shelves, and the producers have been slow to respond to this challenge. Many wines from Burgundy now need to be actively pushed, and that means delving into the mucky world of sales and marketing.

'Selling shit to idiots'

'Marketing', according to one well-known and very vocal burgundy producer, 'is the art of selling shit to idiots'. Those of a kindlier or more polite disposition might balk at such a statement, but the truth is that not every wine is so good that it sells itself, and not every wine-drinker can recite the roster of the World's 1,000 Best Wines. You need only visit a average supermarket to see the vast range of wines available. Faced with an array of 500 labels, it's not surprising that customers plump for a tried and trusted brand, or a wine which is on special offer, or a bottle with particularly striking packaging.

As one of the largest producers in Burgundy, Jadot is a familiar name to wine-lovers. To reinforce what the marketers called 'brand recognition', there is the ubiquitous company motif. This features the head of Bacchus taken from an original carving on a wall of the old Couvent des Jacobins in Beaune, which now houses the company's administrative offices. Castings have been taken from this, and the figure also appears at the entrance to La Sablière. In addition, every bottle of Jadot wine carries its image on the capsule, neck label and main label.

Less established companies have to go to greater lengths to make their wines stand out on the shelf. Recent years have seen many abandon conventional bottles in favour of ones made from expensive Italian glass, sometimes with slightly sloping sides. They can look fabulous, although sometimes their designers make them too tall to fit on standard-sized shop shelves. There are bottles with flanges, or lips, round the top, which again catch the eye, even if they're not always corkscrew-friendly.

Dressed to kill

While flavour and reliability have played a large part in the rising fortunes of wines from New World (non-European) countries, the importance of their user-friendly labels should not be underestimated. This is especially true in English-speaking countries, none of which has a culture of wine drinking. After years of struggling with gothic script and difficult names such as Pernand-Vergelesses, or Carmignano or Trockenbeerenauslese, a wine called simply 'Montana Marlborough Chardonnay' comes as a blessed relief.

Then there's the label design, which in a different book could easily merit a chapter of its own. Indeed, with some wines, it seems

LA BAUME

ROLL UP, ROLL UP
How successful is La Baume in France? 'We haven't really tried to break into the French market so far,' says Ashley. 'The general perception of the Languedoc in France is that it makes large volumes of not particularly good wine. However that is changing. Overall sales of wine here are static, but if you look at them more closely, the Languedoc is taking market share from cheap burgundy and Bordeaux. We're starting to make an impact in the USA, and we send some wine back to Australia, but the UK is our main customer by a long way. Regular sales in large volumes into British supermarkets give us the ability to be able to explore the premium end of the market.'

'...with some wines, it seems that more effort went into designing the packaging than into making the wine it adorns. The phrase "mutton dressed as lamb" springs to mind.'

that more effort went into designing the packaging than into making the wine it adorns. The phrase 'mutton dressed as lamb' springs to mind, but as long as someone is buying one brand of mutton rather than another, then the marketing suits have done their job.

In comparison with many modern wines, the Jadot packaging is sedate, and with the exception of the back labels, which differ according to the country they're destined for, is the same the world over. The wines coming off the bottling line at the end of the last chapter had neither labels nor capsules. They'll be stored like this, stacked up in large wooden containers in a large air-conditioned warehouse at La Sablière, until just before despatch, otherwise the labels might get damaged.

When an order comes in, the container is taken from the warehouse to labelling and packaging machine. If you thought the bottling line was slick, then this contraption is slick to the power of slick. Nude bottles, capsules, labels and cardboard go in at one end and, if the machine is working as it should do, fully packaged cases of wine come out at the other. If it isn't, there's a painful crunching sound, and the smell of wine begins to fill the room.

Keeping it safe and not too warm

The wines are then transferred to a different warehouse ready for shipping. Again the building is air-conditioned. The importance of good storage for wine cannot be over-emphasised. Burgundy, especially if it has not been filtered, is extremely sensitive to fluctuations in temperature, so wines are not only stored but also transported and shipped in temperature-controlled conditions. How the eventual purchaser treats the wine is beyond Jadot's control, but at least Pierre-Henry knows that there will be no heat-related problems along the distribution chain.

While most of the wines will spend only a short time in the two warehouses, a few of them have been around for a little longer, and considerably longer in some instances. Sometimes a supplier never picks up the wine he's ordered, sometimes supply for certain wines can outstrip demand, and sometimes there are even stocks of wines in the warehouse which have simply been forgotten about. There's a range of these on the bench in the lab, and Jacques and Christine are tasting their way through them.

HARDY ANNUAL
'It's undoubtedly a plus point being part of the BRL Hardy organisation,' says Ashley. 'It's not so much the sales into Australia. Selling French wine to Australia is as difficult as selling Australian wine to France. However, they have an excellent worldwide distribution network which is very important. You can say all you want about winemaking, but at the end of the day, you still have to sell what you've made. The only drawback is that the company is now involved in wine ventures in a number of countries, not just Australia, so I have to make sure that my wines are plugged as much as those from other parts of the world!'

Above. To cap it all off. *Neatly stacked capsules wait for their turn on the packaging line*

Below. All dressed and ready to go. *Now in full livery, the bottles just need a box to rest in*

Size is important

Says Jacques: 'We often find ourselves with reasonable supplies of half-bottles long after the full ones have gone. So we taste them, like we are doing today. If they are good, we'll sell them to a restaurant or a merchant we like, but often we just keep them for when we have friends around for lunch'. Ever the maverick, Jacques believes that half-bottles take longer than full-sized ones to reach maturity, which goes right against conventional wisdom. 'But it is obvious, *hein*? The wine undergoes much more of a shock when it goes into the smaller bottle, and so takes more time to come round again.'

Ageing and beauty

Certainly there are wines in the line-up today which testify to the ageing power of half-bottles. There's a superb and still juvenile 1989 Beaune Boucherottes, as well as a 1970 Corton Hospices de Beaune Charlotte Dumas which is also fighting fit. However, a Côtes de Nuits-Villages from the same vintage and a 1966 Clos de la Roche are rather less impressive. Jacques wrinkles up his nose in displeasure. 'It may just be these bottles. We'll try them again some other time soon'. And if they're still not pleasant? He grimaces and points to the sink.

The Clos de le Roche is by no means the oldest wine in the Jadot stores. Each vintage, several dozen bottles of each wine are set aside for storage in the wine 'library' at La Sablière, and these will be pulled out in later years for dinners, tastings and other special events. Beneath the company's administrative offices in the centre of Beaune lies an extensive collection of even older bottles, dating back to an 1845 Clos Vougeot, identifiable only by a tag hanging round its neck. There are stocks from most subsequent vintages, with especially healthy supplies from 1953.

Are these perhaps being kept to celebrate the Queen of England's Golden Jubilee? The lovely Laura, one of those young French women who probably looks immaculate five days into a camping trip, doesn't think so. As her English is excellent, one of her tasks is to show visitors round this impressive collection, and today her guests are a trio of Canadian restaurateurs who have arrived unannounced. They can't get over how these venerable bottles are simply lying on a gravel floor, rather than being housed in a protective cage. Anyone could just grab those last two bottles of

1898 Montrachet and stash them in their bag. 'It doesn't worry us', says Laura. 'Most of our visitors work in the wine business, and we've never had any problems.'

Power of the press

It's August 2000 and Michael Aaron is having problems. He's the boss of the well-known New York retailer Sherry Lehmann, and such is his current disquiet that he's brought his chief salesman with him on his annual trip to Burgundy. The cause for concern is an article in the influential American magazine the *Wine Advocate* which begins, 'Overall, the 1998 vintage for red burgundies is of average to poor quality.' Pierre-Antoine Rovani, the author of the curiously brief appraisal of the vintage, had tasted no wines chez Jadot which had been deemed worthy of an 'outstanding' score of 90 or more points

out of 100. The same was true at dozens of other highly thought of estates, including the famous Domaine de la Romanée-Conti.

Aaron voices his frustration to Jacques and Pierre-Henry. 'I was told that the 1998s were good, so I ordered lots of them, and then this comes out. Now the customers don't want to buy any of them. They've been told they're below average'. Jacques smiles and shrugs. 1998 certainly wasn't the easiest of vintages, with the weather ranging from dismally wet and cold to scorching hot. Those who worked on the sorting table found themselves on occasion discarding as much as they kept. There's plenty he could say, but for the moment his reply is to open a selection of 1998s, both reds and whites, most of which were bottled only the month before. Jacques points out that after bottling, burgundies need at least 12–18 months to 'recover their harmony'. Some seem awkward and

Left. Slightly woody on the pallet...
*Barrel staves in the foreground,
vineyards on the hill of Corton in
the background*

NO RECIPE

Ashley has a dual role at La Baume. 'I manage the business, but I also have to make sure the wine tastes good. I don't want to cut corners in either field. Today, there's no excuse for bad wine whatever the price, but there are still producers who approach the whole job of winemaking with a factory mentality, and the results are correct but bland. Our approach is to make the wine as far as possible on a vineyard by vineyard basis, and while this means more effort on our part, the benefits are tangible.'

disjointed, but others are extremely good, and if the best of them aren't outstanding, it's hard to know what is.

Having let the wines talk first, Jacques now takes over. 'I do not make wine to show well in barrel. Sure, I can do it, but what's the point? It's crazy to judge burgundies on one tasting of barrel samples. Vignerons feel obliged to give excuses – "It's just been bottled, it's going through malo, it's only just been racked, it needs racking" and so on. Here, we make our wines so they reach their peak after they've been bottled, not before. And sure, when you taste them at the wrong time, they can be difficult – I'm aware that many will be drunk even before they've recovered from bottling.'

Aaron and his henchman leave Burgundy feeling happier than when they arrived. Even so, they still reckon that disposing of their quota of 1998 burgundies will be an uphill struggle and that they'll have to hand-sell every bottle. When he's gone, Pierre-Henry smiles. 'America is our most important market, so it's a shame that it is governed to such an extent by what the critics say. All a retailer like Michael Aaron has to do to succeed is buy the wines which get the high scores. But I admire the way that he comes here year after year to taste for himself, and form his own opinions.'

On sale in the village shop!

While it's not possible to roll up to La Sablière and buy a bottle of Chassagne-Montrachet, Jadot has a quarter share in a shop in the main square of Beaune where virtually all the wines are on sale. The importance of the *Wine Advocate* can be seen in the number of loud-shirted American tourists walking round clutching an issue and matching the comments on the page to the bottles on the shelf. Jadot wines also make their presence felt on restaurant lists in the region. Anyone visiting the charming Ma Cuisine just off the square should certainly see whether there is any of the sublime 1981 Puligny-Montrachet Les Referts in the cellar.

But most of the wine leaves the region for sale overseas. The USA is the largest market, receiving around 70 per cent of the total production. Such is the company's success there that every fifth bottle of burgundy sold carries a Jadot label. Pierre-Henry often travels to the States to help promote his wines, sometimes with the voluble Jacques in tow.

The UK is also an important customer. The agent there is Hatch Mansfield, which is owned 50 per cent by Jadot and 50 per cent by

the Chilean producer Viña Errázuriz. Pierre-Henry finds that this relationship works very well. 'In Burgundy, we are sometimes a little blind as to what is going on in other parts of the world. I've visited all the wine-producing countries, which I feel is important, and what impresses me about the New World is that it knows how to be friendly. With the great wines of Burgundy, we are at the mercy of the terroir, but with the simpler wines, we have to listen to what sells. If they are difficult to understand, no one will buy them.'

While Jadot doesn't have the same dominance of the burgundy market in the UK that it enjoys in the USA, the wines enjoy good exposure on the lists of many merchants and restaurants. Each February, Hatch Mansfield holds a tasting at which trade buyers can have a preview of wines before they order them. At the February 2000 event at the London Hilton, it is a selection from the 1998 vintage which is under scrutiny. Some of the wines are in short supply – there are three cases of Chambertin Clos de Bèze up for grabs, for instance – while others are reasonably plentiful.

On display in London

February is a busy month in the London wine tasting calendar. Buyers often find themselves trying to get to three, even four different events in the day, so the time they can spend at each is limited. It's not the ideal way to select wine, but since the alternative is to miss the events altogether, it has to be done.

Some people manage to taste their way around the 40+ wines in less than an hour, before dashing out towards the next tasting. Some give the wines a little more time, while others seem to spend all day there, enjoying the free lunch and in some cases not doing a great deal of spitting.

The general consensus is that the whites show very well, and the three wines from Château des Jacques in Moulin-à-Vent are also impressive. On the other hand, the reds from the Côte d'Or are much more erratic, and there are mutterings that they seem simple and thin. Over lunch, one merchant says, 'I'm going to buy as many whites as I can, and then cherry-pick through the reds', and many at the table nod in agreement.

Best of all, in the cellar

However, six months later in the cellar at La Sablière with Michael Aaron, the same reds taste much better, and seem to have put on weight. What has happened? 'The wines in London were barrel samples', says Pierre-Henry. 'I don't really like doing tastings like that, because you're not seeing a finished wine. It is unnatural. If we could transport the cellar and allow the people to taste straight from the cask, it would be better. But of course we can't.'

Isn't this just making excuses for the wines? 'Maybe, but you have seen for yourself how the wines have changed and improved, and I believe they're going to get even better. That's why when we have visitors, we always open some older wines to reassure them.' Jacques chips in. 'The wines, they always surprise you. They still surprise me, but I like it that way. In order to produce great wine, you have to take risks, and sometimes they work, sometimes they don't. It would be very easy to make wines that were simple and correct, but because I respect the customer, I won't do that. When you aim for the highest level, the reality is that people will not like certain wines.'

Christine bustles up, glass in hand. In it is a blend put together from the 28 healthy casks of 1999 Beaune Boucherottes, and it's wonderfully fragrant and chunky. 'See', says Jacques, stabbing his glass into the air, 'look what has happened here. This blend is much better than any of the individual casks, and they were all different, even though they started off as the same wine. Why, I always ask myself, why? And some day, maybe some day, I will find an answer.'

index

bibliography

The Art & Science of Wine,
James Halliday & Hugh Johnson
(Mitchell Beazley 1992)

Burgundy, Anthony Hanson
(2nd ed. Faber & Faber 1995)

The Great Domaines of Burgundy,
Remington Norman (2nd ed. Kyle
Cathie 1996)

The Oxford Companion to Wine,
edited by Jancis Robinson (2nd ed.
Oxford University Press 1999)